HARMONY IN ACTION

A practical course in tonal harmony

DAVID TUNLEY
Professor of Music, University of Western Australia

FABER MUSIC
London & Boston
IN ASSOCIATION WITH FABER AND FABER

*First published in 1978 by the Department of Music,
University of Western Australia
This revised edition first published in 1984
by Faber Music Limited in association with Faber & Faber Limited
3 Queen Square, London WC1N 3AU
Printed in Great Britain by
BAS Printers Ltd, Over Wallop, Hampshire
All Rights Reserved*

© *David Tunley 1984*

Library of Congress Cataloging in Publication Data

*Tunley, David.
Harmony in action.
1. Harmony.   I. Title.
MT50. T885 1984   781.3   84-13480
ISBN 0-571-10056-2 (pbk.)*

British Library Cataloguing in Publication Data

*Tunley, David
Harmony in action.
1. Harmony
I. Title
781.3   MT50
ISBN 0-571-10056- 2*

ERRATA

p. 21   line 7   VII should read ♭VII
p. 55   line 8   D should read D♭
p. 124 line 3   B should read B♭

To the Memory of Nadia Boulanger (1887-1979)

'IN MY OPINION, IN INSTRUCTING MUSIC-LOVERS, several things could be omitted that many musicians do not, indeed need not know. On the other hand, a most important element, analysis, is lacking. True masterpieces should be taken from all styles of composition, and the music-lover should be shown the beauty, daring and novelty in them. Also, he should be shown how insignificant the piece would be if these things were lacking. Further he should be shown how errors, pitfalls, have been avoided, and especially how far a work departs from ordinary ways, how venturesome it can be.'

C.P.E. BACH (*letter to a friend, 1777*)

CONTENTS

INTRODUCTION		page	7
SYMBOLS FOR HARMONIC ANALYSIS			9
CHAPTER ONE	THE CONCEPT OF TONALITY		11
	Assignments for Chapter One		24
CHAPTER TWO	TEXTURE		31
	Assignments for Chapter Two		40
CHAPTER THREE	DISSONANCE		47
	Assignments for Chapter Three		62
CHAPTER FOUR	CHROMATICISM AND MODULATION		70
	Assignments for Chapter Four		82
CHAPTER FIVE	EXTENSIONS OF THE TRIADIC FOUNDATION		85
	Assignments for Chapter Five		105
CHAPTER SIX	HARMONY IN STRUCTURAL CONTEXT		118
	Assignment for Chapter Six		127
FURTHER READING			128

INTRODUCTION

In recent years the focus of music studies has widened very considerably, often embracing music of non-Western cultures as well as that of the ever-expanding European repertoire. Such a widened scope inevitably forces a reappraisal of those areas which were once the core of serious musical studies; in particular the teaching of tonal harmony.

If viewed in this wide perspective, the repertoire which was based upon the harmonic principles in use during the 17th to 19th centuries (loosely called tonal harmony) is relatively small; yet the significance of that repertoire to European culture cannot be measured in this way, and any course which aims for a balanced view of music must at some time come to serious terms with it. A study of its language as well as its literature is one of the ways of doing it. Nevertheless, pressure from other components of the music course usually restricts what opportunities there are for this, a situation exacerbated when the subject is taken as one of a number of other studies, as in an arts degree or music teacher training course, or at school. Performance courses have similar problems when 'academic' studies are seen as a background to the time-consuming demands of practice. It is hoped that the present textbook will be useful in all these situations.

The elements which the present course brings together are certainly not new: harmonic analysis, some constructive assignments, keyboard and singing exercises and so on. However, it differs from most harmony books in several ways. Recognizing the widened focus of today's studies, the course places the phenomenon of tonality in an historical as much as a technical framework. Thus in contrast to many textbooks which treat the subject as a 'sealed unit', the present one attempts to place such concepts as dissonance and chromaticism in a wider context than usual, and includes a consideration of the relationship between harmony and other elements of musical design.

Believing that the most important discoveries in a student's life are those he makes for himself, I have deliberately left various points 'in the air', providing, in place of explanation, assignments which enable these to be followed up. The question of note-doubling in four-part harmony, for example, is examined not by passing on the usual rules and precepts, but by requiring the student to undertake the discipline of observation, tabulation of results and the formulation of principles suggested by the musical evidence. If this leads him to question traditional textbook rules so much the better. As the present course aims to help the student understand tonal concepts as practised in the masterworks of the period rather than to develop fluency of writing in an outmoded idiom (which is far from saying that the music is outmoded), the purpose of discussing such matters as note-doubling may well be questioned. Yet, not only is it an integral part of one's understanding of texture and sonority, but it is intimately related to voice-leading. In these and other aspects, the aim of the course is, above all, to develop aural sensitivity to the subtle processes which composers exploited in so many original ways. It need hardly be pointed out then that it is essential for all examples and assignments to be played or sung. This course presupposes a thorough knowledge of scales, keys and intervals.

The symbols for harmonic analysis used in this book are described below. They include the sign for 'missing roots', and as this is a somewhat controversial matter, a brief explanation is required. The object of our analysis is to rationalize and elucidate a particular harmonic situation. There are many passages which, while they may look baffling on the page, sound very clear harmonically in performance. The clue to all understanding of such passages can often lie in recognizing that certain chords can behave like dominants even though the dominant root may be absent. In noting, for example, the dominant function of the diminished triad on the leading-note, it becomes merely a matter of semantics as to whether we describe it as a chord functioning as a dominant 7th or as a dominant 7th with missing root. From the point of view of shorthand symbols, such as are used in this book, the latter is less cumbersome. It is true that the actual sonority of a chord is affected (to a greater or lesser degree) by the presence or absence of its root, but this does not necessarily affect its function, i.e. its relationship to the next chord. It is the seeking out of relationships, hidden perhaps to the eye but not to the ear, which raises harmonic analysis above mere description. If, of course, a composer has set out to 'deliberately mystify' (to quote Tovey), then the analysis will be accordingly different. As the object of analysis is to explain the harmonic situation, then if it fails to do this the analysis is worthless. It should be uncluttered and directed to the particular problem at hand. In the present course the analysis is primarily used to communicate, in shorthand, ideas that help the student understand the basic concepts of tonal harmony.

It seems inevitable that a book on harmony emphasizes certain procedures which in performance, particularly of fast music, are less noticeable than textbook discussion would suggest. Yet any course that deals with one aspect of music must place its examples under the microscope, so to speak, resulting in an image somewhat larger than life. Music, however, is a complex of factors of which the harmonic element is only one, and the course must be seen in this light. In order to adjust the perspective the final chapter attempts to place the study of harmony in relation to the other elements.

My thanks go to the many students who for over a decade have, unwittingly, acted as guinea pigs during the compilation of this course and to their tutors who have encouraged me with their advice. Above all, I am deeply indebted to Mrs Margaret Seares, Dr David Symons and Mr Brian Michell of the Department of Music at the University of Western Australia, whose perceptive and critical views have helped me immeasurably in preparing the revised edition of this book.

To Mr Martin Kingsbury of Faber Music I am deeply indebted for the care he has taken in matters both musical and editorial.

DAVID TUNLEY
Department of Music, University of Western Australia

SYMBOLS FOR HARMONIC ANALYSIS

The analytical method used in this course employs symbols related to the *root* of each chord. It is thus totally different from 'figured bass' in which the symbols indicate chordal structure by intervals measured from the *bass*. To illustrate the difference, here is a chord (the tonic 7th) in all its positions, the two kinds of figuring shown underneath:

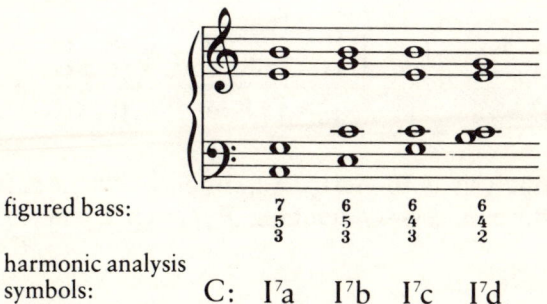

Of the two, the harmonic analysis symbols indicate the nature of the chord far more clearly and simply than does figured bass. On the other hand, it depends upon an unequivocal statement of key; if the key is not clearly defined it is difficult to choose a symbol to represent the chord. Hence the system is often impracticable in some of Wagner's music, and breaks down entirely in Debussy's. The key of the passage is indicated by A (major), a (minor), etc.

SYMBOLS

(a) large roman numeral: chord with major 3rd & perfect 5th from root, i.e. a major chord.

(b) small roman numeral: chord with minor 3rd & perfect 5th from root, i.e. a minor chord.

(c) o: the interval of the 5th from the root is diminished.

(d) +:   the interval of the 5th from the root is augmented.

(e) 4, 6, 7, 9, 11, 13:   intervals of these sizes added from the root. The most usual are 7 & 9.

(f) ♭ or ♯ before these numerals: chromatic alteration of intervals 4, 6, etc.

(g) ♭ or ♯ before the *roman* numeral: root of the chord has been chromatically lowered or raised.

(h) a, b, c, d, etc.:   position of the chord (a = root position; b = 1st inversion). However, it is usually only necessary to use these for inversions, the roman numeral by itself implying root position.

(i) ⚡ :   missing root (usually a dominant root), the sign to be placed on the relevant line or space on the stave.

EXAMPLES

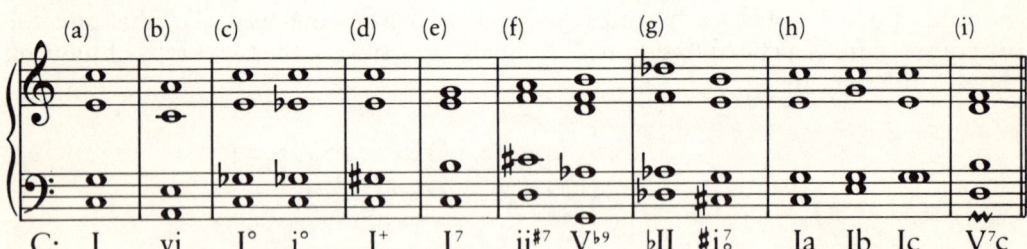

As the purpose of analysis is to clarify a harmonic situation, it is not desirable to clutter the work with unnecessary symbols. Experience will show how far to go in this.

CHAPTER ONE
THE CONCEPT OF TONALITY

MODALITY AND TONALITY

In striking contrast to much non-Western music, that of Europe from medieval times to the present day has been characterized by constant change. Yet through its rich variety of expression runs an unmistakable thread of continuity which not only prompts us to recognize affinities between strongly contrasted works within a system of musical organization, but which also shows us the evolutionary nature of the systems themselves.

The system known as tonality emerged during the early years of the 17th century, and such was its potential that it took three centuries of composition to exhaust. Although this is a relatively short period compared to that occupied by the previous system – modality – during this time were composed the majority of works which are most familiar to concert audiences today. Yet there is now also a growing appreciation and cultivation of music outside the tonal system – that from our own century, the more distant past and from other cultures. More than at any other time, we are able to savour something of the universality of musical experience and in so doing view the music of the 17th to the 19th centuries in a wider focus.

We will thus commence our study by comparing a work from the period of modality in its final phase with one from the period of tonality in its middle phase. Play (or sing) these works several times.

EX.1 (a) Palestrina: *Missa Aeterna Christi Munera,* (1590)

EX. 1 (b) Chorale: *Werde munter, mein Gemüte* (harmonized by J. A. Hiller, 1793)

These two works have been chosen because they have certain features in common: both are chordal or homophonic in texture and (as we shall see) both employ similar chordal structures. Yet in performance their differences are more striking than their similarities. In particular, while the second piece generates a firm sense of key-centre (F major, with modulations that highlight its eventual return), the first is seemingly less stable. Palestrina's work is indeed not based upon a key, but upon a mode.

Up to the end of the 16th century most Western European music was based upon the 'church' modes. Medieval and renaissance theorists, following ancient Greek terminology, called these modes Dorian, Phrygian, Lydian, Mixolydian, Aeolian and Ionian (see Ex.2).

EX.2

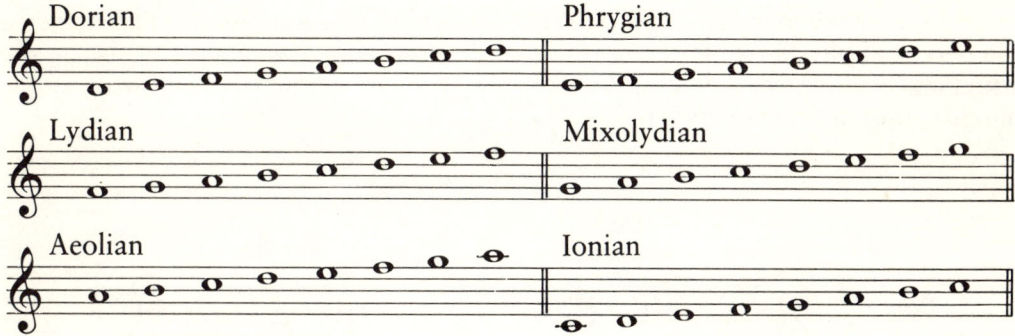

They could also be used in one transposed form: up a perfect 4th (or down a perfect 5th). In this case B♭ was placed at the beginning of each staff. Thus the B♭ at the beginning of Palestrina's piece is not the key signature of F major but the sign of a transposed mode. This system which served music so admirably for many centuries has been called by modern theorists the system of 'modality'.

A growing tendency, particularly towards the end of the period, to alter chromatically certain notes of the modes (especially the 7th degree at cadence points)[1] blurred the outlines of the modes and reduced the system eventually to two scalic forms which were to become known as major and minor (Ex.3). This became the basis of what is usually called 'tonality'.

EX.3

[1] The practice of chromatic alteration was known as *musica ficta*. In passing we should note that the Phrygian mode maintained its individuality, because of the reluctance of composers to sharpen the 7th.

Palestrina's piece is especially useful in our study of emerging tonality. It will have been noted that one of the modes, the Ionian, was identical with the scale of C major. Palestrina's *Missa Aeterna Christi Munera* from which our extract comes is in fact based on the Ionian mode in its *transposed* version, the notes of this mode being identical with the scale of F major. Yet, unlike the chorale at Ex.1(b), the piece in no way sounds as if it were in the *key* of F major. We will examine the reason for this shortly, but before doing so it will be necessary to define some terms.

The Triadic Basis and the Theory of Inversions
In synchronizing their parts the voices in Ex.1(a) and 1(b) produce in both cases a series of vertical relationships or chords that can theoretically be reduced to a triadic structure comprising a major or minor 3rd and a perfect or diminished 5th above a 'root' note or the inversion of these intervals below it. (Although not illustrated in the two examples, an augmented 5th from the root may also be part of the triadic structure.) Taking the opening bars of each we can extract the following triads (circled notes indicate the root):

EX.4

In the early 18th century the French composer and theorist Jean-Philippe Rameau, attempting to rationalize the musical practice of his day, proposed the idea that when the notes of a triad in 'root position' are re-arranged so that the root is no longer the bass, the resulting triads can be identified as being inversions of the root position triad. Thus the second and third triads of the next example are the same as the first but in 1st and 2nd inversion respectively.

EX.5

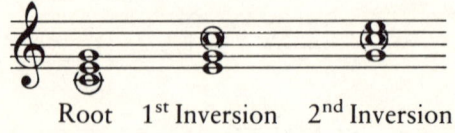

The Theory of Inversions, as it is called, sounds very logical and is still the basis of most traditional harmony teaching today. Yet musical theory and practice do not always agree. For example, there is a context in which the third chord of Ex.5

sounds less like a C major triad and more a harmonic decoration of a G major triad, as in Ex.6 where it is indicated by an asterisk.

EX.6 Mozart: *Piano Sonata in C, K309*

This is no reason why the Theory of Inversions should be abandoned, but it is a reminder that theory and practice do not always come together. As one of the main purposes of our study is to determine the *function* of a particular chord, our analyses must always be validated by the ear.

The vertical structure can be extended further by adding superimposed thirds producing chords which, because of the size of the added interval from the root, are known as chords of the 7th, 9th, 11th and 13th (Ex.7):

EX.7

To view them this way, however, is to remove them from musical reality, for these dissonant chords are invariably the result of contrapuntal movement, and brought about by the use of suspensions, passing notes and other forms of dissonance treatment discussed in Chapter Three. Only the chord later known as the dominant 7th achieved a degree of independence from contrapuntal associations. Yet, as we shall see, even this mild chord was subject to certain restrictions which prevent it from being regarded as an 'entity' (until the time of Debussy and the disintegration of tonality).

The contrapuntal origin of all chordal structures, whether dissonant or not, explains why most of the so-called rules of harmony are in fact rules of counterpoint.

By recognizing the triadic basis of modality and tonality (keeping in mind all the time that these chordal structures are the vertical result of horizontal or linear movement) we can now begin to examine the Palestrina extract and the chorale in more detail and see why, although they are based on similar harmonic material, they sound very different.

The Dominant/Tonic Relationship

As mentioned earlier, one of the characteristics of the chorale is its clear definition of key-centres: F major with brief modulations (key changes) to G minor and B♭ major. We shall see how this definition is achieved.

As the analysis below indicates, tonic and dominant chords permeate the harmony; out of 29 chords, 19 are of this kind.

EX.8

What is more, these two chords tend to be coupled together and form a relationship in which the tonic is felt to be a kind of magnet drawing the dominant to it. This relationship is the generator of tonality. While Palestrina's piece (Ex.1a) commences with triads built upon roots C F C, after this the relationship disappears until towards the end when it returns as a V – I cadence on G. Its absence partly explains why this work has less of a tonal feel about it than the chorale.

The Dominant 7th

The function of the dominant triad becomes even more compelling when a minor 7th from the root is added. The intervallic structure of the dominant 7th is thus: major 3rd from root, perfect 5th from root, minor 7th from root. (Memorize this structure.)

EX.9

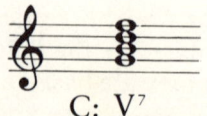

It will be seen that the dominant 7th contains the tritone (augmented 4th or diminished 5th) and it is the presence of this restless interval which seems to urge the chord to resolve in the following way:

EX.10   EX.11

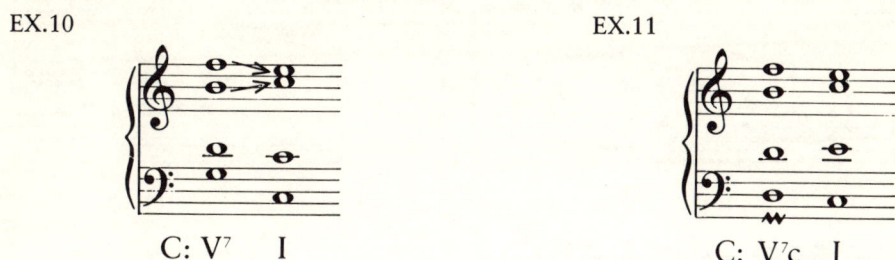

So strong is the force of the tritone in this context that the dominant 7th does not even need the root to establish its *function* (Ex.11; here the 'missing root' G is indicated by the symbol , explained on p.10).

Certainly the first chord in Ex.11 could be analysed as vii°, but in practice the chord on the leading-note usually functions as a dominant 7th with missing root. As the purpose of harmonic analysis is to understand chordal functions, where appropriate, vii° chords will be analysed as V^7 to clarify the harmonic logic. (On the other hand there are also times when vii° functions as a triad in its own right, as for example, in the Cycle of 5ths which will be discussed later in this chapter.)

Conventional resolutions of the dominant 7th are:

EX.12

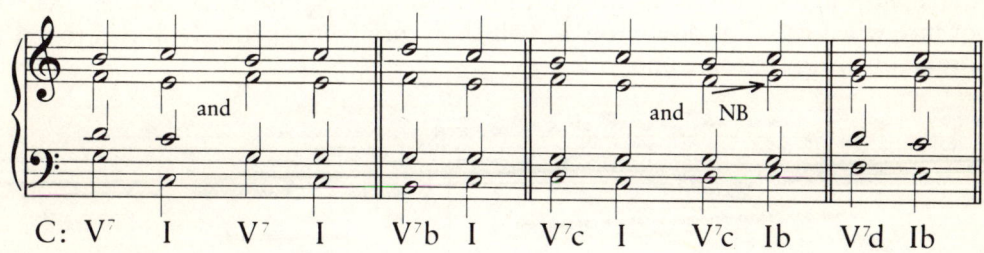

Note that the 7th always falls, except in V^7c to Ib as indicated above.

We will now analyse the opening of Bach's Prelude in F♯ minor from the second book of the 48 Preludes and Fugues. But before doing so it is suggested that you resolve the different positions of the dominant 7th in F♯ minor following the pattern set out at Ex. 12. (You should also play these at the piano.) Compare these resolutions with the way Bach has transformed them into music and observe how the same principles of resolution are at work.

EX.13 J. S. Bach: *Prelude No. 14, Preludes and Fugues, Book II*

These processes of resolution illustrate a feature of tonality. The key sets up a kind of harmonic 'field' in which subtle forces are at work. Some notes are particularly susceptible to these forces, like the E♯ which is drawn (as though magnetically) to F♯. The interplay of forces gives to tonal music much of its logic and expressive power; composers have responded to it intuitively (as do we listeners if we are in any way conditioned to this style of music), and they often exploited effects that are dramatic or highly expressive because these very forces have been resisted. See, for example, how in a later passage from the same work the phrase achieves even greater eloquence when E♯ dips down to B♯ (which in turn is magnetically drawn to C♯) before resolving to the tonic note (F♯).

One of the most telling passages in 18th-century music comes from Mozart's Fantasia in C minor. Our expectations of the normal resolution of the following dominant 7ths are:

EX.15

They are thwarted by Mozart's music which, shaped by the sequential development of the work's opening motive (now in the bass), leads to progressions the originality of which is related to their *avoidance* of conventional syntax. Note in this work also how a feeling of key stability enters the music with the conventional resolutions of the dominant 7th at bar 6.

EX.16 Mozart: *Fantasia in C minor, K457*

In the dominant/tonic relationship lie the seeds of tonality. It is no mere coincidence that what affinities we feel between the Palestrina extract and the chorale (quoted at Ex.1) occur at those points in the Palestrina where this relationship is established: the opening (F: V – I) and closing (g: V – I) and also at bar 9 where the diminished triad functions like a dominant 7th in F, with missing root (Ex.17).

EX.17

(F: V⁷c   I)

If in much modal music this relationship is seen mainly at cadence points (whether they be on the 'final' of the mode, i.e. D in Dorian, etc, or on other degrees of the mode), in tonality the dominant/tonic relationship is constantly in evidence.

Extension of the Dominant/Tonic Relationship and the Cycle of 5ths
It will have been noted that the dominant to tonic progression involves the root movement of a perfect 5th downwards (or a perfect 4th upwards). In connecting these two chords such root movement has become associated with a strong, unequivocal statement. In the chorale (Ex.1(b)) it is at work at the cadence and in progressions leading up to some cadences, as for example, at the closing bars.

EX.18

Root movement

These root movements illustrate how chord ii bears the same relationship to V as V does to I. Similarly the relationship between vi and ii. The strength of these relationships is very clearly perceived in performance (which in any case is the only criterion). By extending the dominant/tonic relationship to all triads in a key we can see the relationship they bear to each other in their strongest context:

EX.19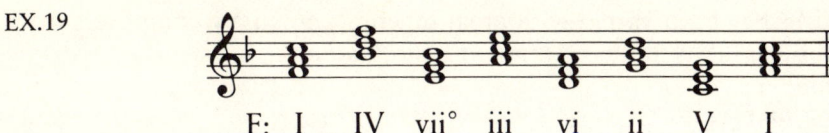

In this so-called Cycle of 5ths one of the root movements (linking IV and vii°) is a diminished 5th, an irregularity which is essential to maintain the key and one which our ear absorbs as part of the pattern. In the minor key, because of the instability of the sixth and seventh notes of the scale, the irregularity can occur in different places. The most common form of the Cycle of 5ths in the minor key (here in F minor for comparison with Ex.19) is as follows:

EX.20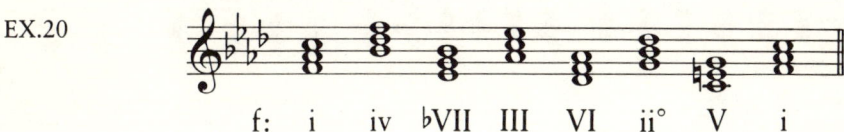

We can see from these two examples of the Cycle of 5ths that while VII plays its part in the definition of a *minor* key it has no role at all in the *major*. Hence in the Palestrina extract the E♭ triad immediately weakens any sense of tonality that might have been generated by the dominant-tonic progression at the opening.

But perhaps the most important thing we learn from the Cycle of 5ths is that in tonality a relationship between the triads, more clearly defined than in modality, is established: a hierarchical relationship at the pinnacle of which stands the tonic triad of the particular key. The assertion of key, the relationship between triads and the potential for modulation gives to tonal music much of its character and logic.

To illustrate the use of a complete Cycle of 5ths in a musical context here is an extract from Bach's third Partita.

EX.21 J. S. Bach: *Partita No. 3*

The Cycle of 5ths has been varied with great ingenuity by many composers often with chromatic inflections as in this opening of Fauré's song:

EX.22 Fauré: *Après un rêve*

The Cycle of 5ths is the most important of the different progressions which constitute a recognizable 'syntax' of tonal harmony. The following progressions also form part of this syntax (only the major key symbols are given below; for minor keys the symbols need adjustment):

    Roots falling a 3rd: I – vi – IV – ii
    Root rising a 3rd: I – iii (other examples are rare)
    Root falling a 2nd: vi – V
    Root rising a 2nd: V – vi (interrupted cadence formula)
        IV – V
        iii – IV
        I – ii^7 (rare without the 7th)
    Root rising a 5th   I – V
    (or falling a 4th):   IV – I (plagal cadence formula)

Two very common formulae:
1) Roots falling a 3rd and rising a 4th: I – vi – ii – vii° – iii, etc.
2) Roots falling or rising by step in 1st inversions, eg: Ib – vii°b – vib – Vb, etc.

These few progressions comprise most of the harmonic 'clichés' which great composers transformed into memorable utterances.

Harmonic Rhythm
We will conclude this study of the concept of tonality by returning to our initial examples, for there remains an element of tonality which is thrown into strong relief by the extract from Palestrina and the chorale. It will have been noted that the unfolding of harmonies in the latter work is far more closely tied to its underlying rhythmic metre, and is far less supple in its flow than is Palestrina's piece. The rhythmic organization of harmony in tonal music is called 'harmonic rhythm' and it plays an important part in the structure of a work. That of the chorale is very simple: an unchanging rate of one chord every beat, lending to the music an even tread that seems to lead compellingly to each cadence. On the other hand there is no *pattern* of chordal change discernible in Palestrina's example.

Two important points emerge from this comparison. One is that through the organization of chordal flow in tonality, harmony tends to direct and absorb the other musical elements, whereas in modality the contrapuntal element assumed this dominating role. The second point is that it reminds us that music is a temporal art: it is concerned with the organization of sounds over a span of time. Only by recognizing this can we understand its full implications.

Assignments for Chapter One

1 (a) Analyse the intervals in the following triads in C major and C minor, *calculating them in each case from the root.*

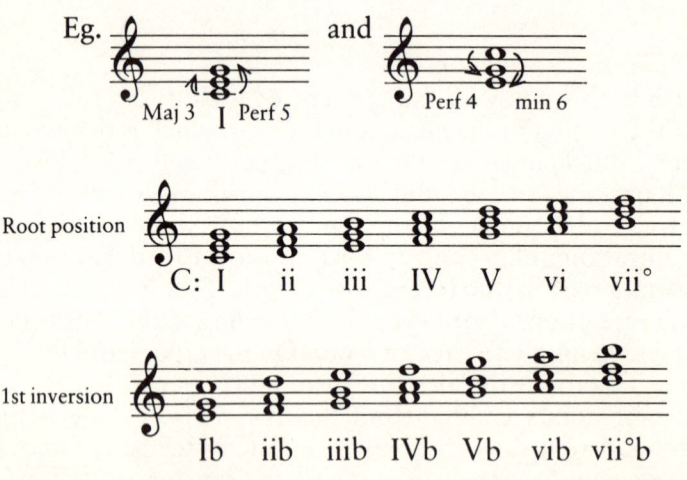

(b) Using the above as a model, write out the triadic resources of at least 3 major keys (other than F major) and 3 minor keys:
1) root position
2) 1st inversion
3) 2nd inversion – tonic (I) only

In minor keys the accidentals and analysis symbols require particular care.

2 (a) On the piano play all the root position triads of C major and C minor, as set out above, and sing the notes of each one thus:

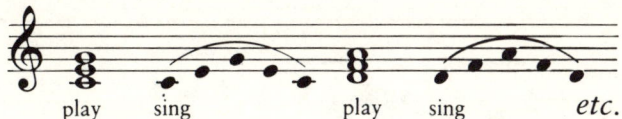

Accuracy of pitch is essential: transpose the starting note down, if required, to suit your voice.

(b) Sing all the root position triads of C major and C minor, playing only the *first* note of each.

3 (a) Write out the triadic resources of F major, G minor and B♭ major (root position and 1st inversion) *using the key signature of F major throughout*. Some of the triads in G minor and B♭ major will require accidentals.

(b) Write out the triadic progressions of the Chorale, Ex.8 on p.16. All the triads required will have been encountered in (a) above. The analysis symbols under each bass note give you the necessary harmonic framework. Begin as follows, and continue to write the analysis symbols under each triad.

4 Analyse the harmonic structure of the following two songs by Schumann, placing analysis symbols beneath the bass notes. Regard the pieces as being in D minor and B minor respectively and without any modulations. The positions (root position, inversions) are determined, of course, by the left hand of the accompaniment.

Schumann: *Liederkreis, Op. 24, No. 8*

Schumann: *Die feindlichen Brüder*, Op. 49, No. 3

b:

5 This assignment is based upon the opening of the famous slow movement of Beethoven's Pathétique Sonata.

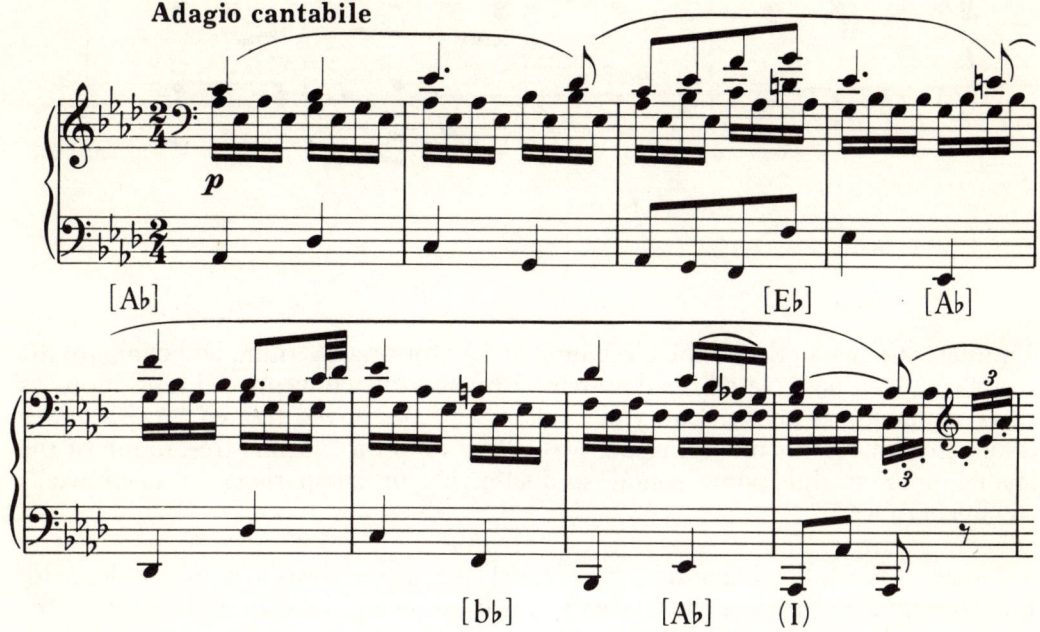

(a) Taking Ex.12 (p.17) as a model, resolve all positions of the dominant 7th in the keys of A♭ major, E♭ major and B♭ minor, using the key signature of four flats for them all. (Accidentals will therefore have to be used in the last two sets of resolutions.)

(b) Using harmonic analysis symbols underneath the left-hand part, show the harmonic basis of this piece (bar 5 is ambiguous). In order to establish the dominant/tonic relationship evident throughout, analyse the chords in the keys indicated on the score.
(c) Examine Beethoven's keyboard writing in this piece and notice how the semiquaver figures suggest 'lines' or 'voices', the whole making up a four-part texture of soprano (Beethoven's melody), alto, tenor, bass.

Translate the remainder of the piece into similar four-part writing and compare the way Beethoven has treated the dominant 7ths with the conventional resolutions as worked out in (a) above. Can you explain why Beethoven treated the B♭ minor dominant 7th (bar 6) in an unusual way? Why does the 'normal' resolution of the leading-note at this point sound so ineffective in comparison to Beethoven's treatment of it?

6   Analyse the following sonata by Handel, placing analysis symbols underneath the bass stave and tracing the Cycle of 5ths by showing the root movement on the extra stave. It is in A minor throughout.

7 (a) Play the following sequence at the piano. Name the chords as you play them and note carefully the movement of each part (sing each from memory). Then transpose the pattern to the keys of G and F major. If you are not a pianist, write out the transpositions before attempting to play them.

C: I   IV   vii°   iii   vi   ii   V   I

(b) Make this progression the basis of an artistic sequential passage for violin and keyboard. You may extend the given opening or use your own ideas. Employ only root position and 1st inversion chords.

8 Write out the root movements of Ex.8 on p.16 (these are not necessarily the bass notes). Check that each root progression can be found as part of the Cycle of 5ths or in the list of common progressions on p.23. The opening is as follows:

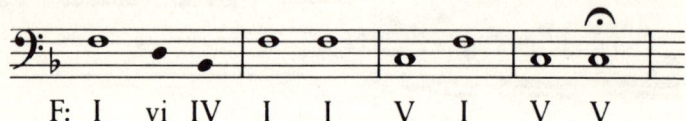

F: I   vi IV   I   I   V   I   V   V

CHAPTER TWO
TEXTURE

The term 'texture', borrowed from the plastic arts, is usefully applied to music although a neat definition of it is difficult to make. Musical texture is concerned with levels of tonal density, whether the music unfolds in contrapuntal or chordal fashion, and whether it is presented in a continuous or fragmentary way. It is also related to instrumental and vocal sonorities, to niceties of balance, and in performance to articulation. It might thus be regarded as a 'surface' feature of the material, but in addition it plays its part in the structure of a composition.

The following extracts from Beethoven's 32 Variations for piano are built upon the tonic and dominant triads of C minor. Play these extracts slowly, focusing your aural attention upon their contrasting textures:

EX.23 Beethoven: *32 Variations in C minor*

(a) Allegretto

(b) Variation I

(c) Variation II

(d) Variation III

(e) Variation VI

(f) Variation VIII

(g) Variation XXIII

When playing these extracts it is essential to observe meticulously all points of articulation (staccato, legato, rests, phrasing, dynamics) for they shape the music's texture. For example, if the theme (Ex.23 (a)) were played legato and the quaver rest omitted, not only would the character of the music be altered but the texture would also be denser and heavier. In most classical, romantic and contemporary scores the texture is usually clearly mirrored in the notation. In baroque works, however, notation can sometimes be misleading, the texture being lighter than the scores suggest. In string music, for example, a more detached style of bowing employed in those days (and recreated in stylish performances today) led to a more 'aerated' texture, particularly in the Allegro movements of Italian music. Clearly, texture is closely related to style.

The possibilities of changing the texture of a single triad were exploited seemingly to the ultimate by Wagner in his Prelude to *Das Rheingold* where the chord of E♭ is extended in time through 136 bars of slow-moving music. You should listen to this, first as a purely aural experience, and then with the orchestral score to gain insight into the extraordinary technical feat accomplished in this famous passage.

Four-Part Writing
Some of the questions relating to texture are seen at their most fundamental in four-part vocal writing. Here the composer must decide which of the three notes of the triad is the best one to double in order to produce effective four-part music. If it were a question of sonority only, the matter would be simple. But the vertical element (the chord) is only one part of the warp and woof of musical texture; the horizontal element is just as important. Four-part writing (or any number of parts for that matter) is essentially a compromise between the demands of sonority, chord progression, the melodic logic of each part (often known as 'voice-leading') and the relationship of each part to the others.

To understand how this works in practice let us examine a simple four-part chorale harmonization by one of J. S. Bach's pupils, G. A. Homilius.

EX.24 Chorale: *Wer nur den lieben Gott lässt walten* (harm. Homilius)

Note-doubling

First of all we shall analyse the note-doubling of all root-position chords, tabulating the results below. All intervals will be calculated from the root, and we shall equate a 3rd with a 10th, etc. With chords of the 7th the question of doubling may not arise as there are four notes in such chords.

DOUBLED (AND TREBLED) ROOT	DOUBLED MAJ 3RD	DOUBLED MIN 3RD	DOUBLED 5TH

We will repeat the process for *1st inversion* chords, again calculating all intervals from the root.

DOUBLED ROOT	DOUBLED MAJ 3RD	DOUBLED MIN 3RD	DOUBLED 5TH

Similarly, the process for *2nd inversion* chords.

DOUBLED ROOT	DOUBLED MAJ 3rd	DOUBLED MIN 3rd	DOUBLED 5th

Clearly this is too small a sampling from which to draw many conclusions — an assignment at the end of this chapter will provide more evidence for these — but there is no doubt that in root-position chords the most commonly doubled note was the root. In practice the doubled major 3rd in root-position chords was not employed as frequently as the present chorale might suggest[1] and certainly not to the exclusion of the doubled 5th.

Its presence in Homilius' piece is associated (with one exception at bar 17) with the progression V – vi (VI) and was normal practice in this context. It leads us to another consideration.

Horizontal Movement
An examination of the four strands which make up the harmony of Ex.25 reveals that, while the soprano part unfolds in shapely spans, and the bass draws strength from a combination of leaps and stepwise movement, the middle voices are relatively unadventurous. This is fairly typical of inner-part movement (even in orchestral and piano music), the repeated or sustained notes and the stepwise movement tending to lend coherence to harmonic flow. Only in truly contrapuntal music, or at moments where a snatch of imitation is heard, a counter-melody drawn or a dramatic point

---

[1] The doubled major 3rd was in fact forbidden by some theorists, a prohibition however which may well have sprung from problems encountered in certain systems of keyboard tuning before equal temperament was fully accepted.

made in a middle voice, does this part of the texture achieve much prominence. Such gentle movement, however, is not to be confused with dullness. Notes held or repeated in the midst of shifting harmonies subtly change character; a chromatic inflection in an inner part may flood a chord with new light. As an illustration sing middle C as a sustained note while playing the following extract from Chopin (Ex.25). As musical eloquence owes much to the subtle beauties of inner-part movement, you should aim to develop sensitivity toward it, either as performer or listener.

EX.25 Chopin: *Prelude in E minor*

To return to the chorale. At bar 3 there is an F major triad with the major 3rd (A) doubled. If the preferred sonority in root-position chords was that in which the root was doubled, why was the A doubled instead of the F? The preferred sonority *could* have been achieved by the tenor doubling the bass on F, thus:

EX.26

To arrive at this chord the tenor must jump from G♯ to F, an interval of an augmented 2nd which, although effective in tense and dramatic music,[1] is inappropriate for an inner part of this simple chorale. Similarly, if the tenor were to double the 5th to effect another sonority the resulting interval of the diminished 4th would be just as inappropriate in this context.

EX.27

[1] For example in the violin obbligato to the aria *Erbarme dich, mein Gott*, No. 47 of Bach's St Matthew Passion.

The same chord appears at bar 7, again with the doubled major 3rd. Here it would have been possible by re-arranging tenor and alto to double the root:

EX.28   bar 7   Original   Altered

One can only assume that Homilius preferred the tonal logic of repeating A and C in the inner parts.

We have seen how the tenor line avoided the augmented 2nd and diminished 4th, the poignancy and tension of these intervals being quite out of character in the bland flow of harmonies and unobtrusive part-writing. To ears conditioned by tonality the 'natural' resolution of G♯ in Exx.26 and 27 is to A, i.e. the leading-note moving to the tonic in a dominant chord progression. As we saw in Chapter One the 7th of the dominant 7th is also very susceptible to tonal forces, its resolution generally being by a downward step. As well as these particular diatonic notes,[1] all chromatic inflections are susceptible to similar tonal forces, as though drawn magnetically up or down a step. The opening of Wagner's Prelude to *Tristan* is a classic example.

EX.29 Wagner: *Prelude to Tristan und Isolde*

Returning to the chorale, the final point to be made concerns bars 16–17. It will be seen that while D (tenor) moves to C, as one might anticipate in dominant 7th resolutions, the leading-note G♯ (alto) does not rise to A as expected, falling instead to E. In preferring to incorporate the 5th in the final chord at the expense of the leading-note's normal resolution, Homilius' harmonization illustrates the essential compromise between the demands of sonority and the demands of melodic logic.

---

[1] That is, notes belonging to a particular major, harmonic or melodic minor scale.

Relationship of each part to the other
The compromise exemplified in part-writing is taken further if we return to bar 3. It might be thought that in the interests of smooth inner-part movement the tenor, in place of jumping from A to D, could have proceeded by step to B:

EX.30

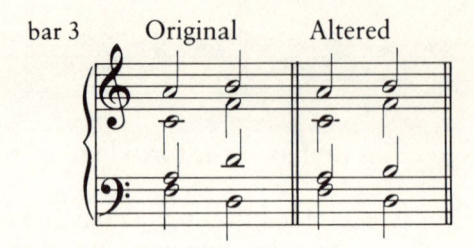

It will be seen that in doing so the tenor follows the same notes (an octave lower) as the melody. The weakness of one voice merely duplicating a few notes of another lies in that the four-part writing momentarily becomes three-part. This must not be confused, however, with the technique of 'doubling' found in orchestral music where the basic four-part framework is *strengthened* through various instrumental duplications or in much piano music where bass or melody is often given out in octaves. But if these give strength to the music, the momentary duplication of one part by another in a four-part texture (as in Ex.30) is the reverse. The flaw is called consecutive octaves.

The relationship of one part to the others has also to be considered in terms of another procedure avoided by composers from renaissance times to the end of the tonal era. If, for example, Homilius' harmonization were altered in bar 11 as follows (Ex.31), the two perfect 5ths produced by bass and alto would be termed consecutive 5ths:

EX.31

Like all musical procedures there is nothing inherently 'wrong' about consecutive 5ths; the question is simply of their stylistic appropriateness. Much of the dynamic strength of medieval music is drawn from them, as in this opening of a rondeau by Adam de la Halle (c.1230–87):

EX.32 Adam de la Halle: *Tant con je vivrai*

Just as the rugged style of medieval architecture, sculpture and painting softened into the smoother contours and textures of renaissance art, so music, too, began to shed some of the earlier characteristics, and with them disappeared (amongst other things) the use of consecutive 5ths. They were to re-appear as an integral part of musical technique only in the late 19th and early 20th centuries when composers like Debussy, Ravel, Vaughan Williams, Holst and others exploited these characteristic sonorities.

A further refinement was observed by the avoidance (as far as the outer parts were concerned) of leaping in similar motion to an octave or 5th:

EX.33

Textbooks mystifyingly call these procedures either 'hidden' or 'exposed' consecutives. While some such progressions do indeed produce weak sounding results, in other contexts they are scarcely noticeable.

Except for some elementary 'construction' assignments at the end of this chapter, questions of consecutives and so on will not concern us overmuch. The aim of the course is not so much to develop a 'composer's' technique in this idiom of the past, but to study in an analytical and practical way the harmonic principles upon which were based the masterworks of the tonal period. Nevertheless it is essential to be aware of the restrictions of the idiom, if for no other reason than to recognize where composers have gone beyond them.

Chord Progression
It was pointed out earlier in this chapter that effective part-writing is a compromise between the demands of sonority, the melodic logic of each part, the relationship of each part to the others and chord progression. The relationship between chord progression (or harmonic syntax) and other elements of musical design will become clearer as the course proceeds.

Assignments for Chapter Two

1   The following accompaniment to Schubert's song *Wohin* provides an example of inner-part movement in characteristic piano texture. Note how the different 'levels' of the arpeggio figuration suggest part-writing. Take each of these levels and trace their melodic lines by *singing* each one as you play the full accompaniment.

Moderato

hin - ab zum Tha - le rau - - schen so frisch und wun - der - hell   Ich weiss nicht wie mir

[musical notation: vocal line with text "wur- de, nicht wer den Rath mir gab, ich muss- te_ auch hin-" with piano accompaniment]

[musical notation: "level 1 level 2 level 3 (see bar 1)"]

After you have become familiar with these inner 'hidden' melodies through singing them, play the accompaniment (or listen to a good pianist play it) with aural awareness of the subtle texture.

2   Using the given opening, compose a piano piece called *The Hunt* employing only the notes of the G major triad (i.e. no other notes except G B D are to appear in it). The object of the assignment is to explore the different keyboard textures possible in a single chord. It must be at least 12 bars long and exhibit shape and a sense of direction. *All details of articulation and dynamics must be considered and set down meticulously in the notation.*

[musical notation: Allegretto, 6/8, pp]

3 (a) Using the same method set out on p.34 analyse the note-doubling procedures of the following chorales:

  (i) *Werde munter, meine Gemüte* (p.12)
  (ii) *Wer nur den lieben Gott lässt walten* (Bach's harmonization), first 7 bars (p.77). Ignore any of the crotchets which do not form part of a triadic structure.

Add these statistics to those from your analysis of Homilius' harmonization of *Wer nur den lieben Gott lässt walten,* and then formulate a set of 'rules' or guide-lines about note-doubling in four-part vocal writing. Make a note in your statistics when the doubled major 3rd is associated with V – VI.

  (b) Study the vertical spacing between soprano and alto, alto and tenor, tenor and bass. Can you observe any principles at work here?

  (c) Why are the leading note and the sub-dominant note rarely doubled in $V^7 – I$? In the progression Ic – V why is the bass (or 5th) of the 2nd inversion doubled?

4 Provide a continuo accompaniment to this dance using two notes only in the right hand. The keyboard part should be harmonically complete, i.e. the three notes of the triad should be sounded where possible; *in no circumstances may the 3rd of the triad be absent in the keyboard part.* The dominant 7th however is a four-note chord, and in the three-part harmony of your accompaniment one note will have to be omitted. Let your ear guide you in this. Aim for smoothness where the harmony changes, and of course check to ensure that there are no consecutives. Do not allow the keyboard part to go above the melody, nor merely reproduce the latter in your accompaniment. Keep the keyboard part simple, avoiding any quaver movement, but nevertheless introduce textural variety by setting out the right-hand notes differently when the melody is repeated from bar 5.

5 (a) Following the principles of note-doubling (for which you have formulated some guide-lines) and spacing deduced from your analyses, add alto, tenor and bass parts to the following phrases taken from chorale melodies. You will have to watch for consecutives at the change of harmony.

(i) Root-position chords only. Do not introduce any notes outside the given triad. Provide *two* versions of each to show textural variety.

G: I I I V I   E♭: I I   I I I IV I   d: i i i i i V i

(ii) 1st and 2nd inversion chords. *One* version will suffice.

Ia Ia Ib Ia Vb Ia   Ia Ia Ib Ib Ia Ia IVa Ib   ia ia ib ib ic V ia

(b) (i) Add a tenor part to the first phrase and an alto part to the second phrase of the harmonization (by Bach) of *Wer weiss, wie nahe mir*. Use only crotchets.

g: i   i Vb i   V   VI   ii°b V   V   B♭: iii vi⁷ Vb   I   {IV
                                                              g:{VI   ic   V   i

(ii) Reconstruct the second violin and viola parts of this early string quartet by Haydn. The rhythmic figure 𝄽𝅘𝅥𝅯𝅘𝅥𝅯𝅘𝅥𝅯 is to be maintained by both instruments throughout. The symbols indicate Haydn's harmonies which you must reproduce. Take care in the resolutions of dominant 7ths, even though Haydn resolved the final one with consecutive octaves!

Haydn: *String Quartet, Op. 1, No. 2*

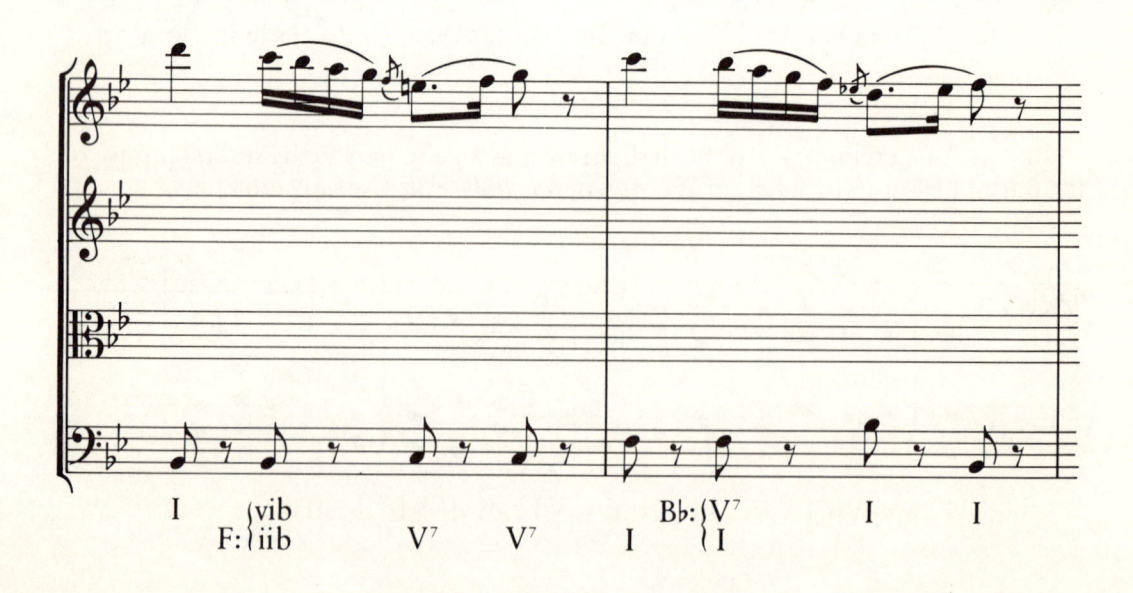

6 Arrange this extract from an aria by Mozart for unaccompanied SATB choir. Keep the voices in comfortable registers and aim for smooth writing in the two inner parts. Each part must be written to fit the words, and Mozart's harmony must be retained at all times. Begin as follows:

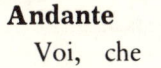

Don - ne, ve - de - te, s'io t'ho nel cor,

7 Analyse the harmony of the following, placing symbols underneath the bass stave:

Beethoven: *Piano Sonata in E♭, Op. 31, No. 3*

SCHERZO
Allegretto vivace

CHAPTER THREE
DISSONANCE

GENERAL CONSIDERATIONS

'Consonance and dissonance are the very foundation of harmonic music, in which the former represents the element of normalcy and repose, the latter the no less important element of irregularity and disturbance.' – Harvard Dictionary of Music.

In the history of European musical style it would be difficult to find extended examples in which dissonance (according to the concept of it at the time) was absent. Even in some of the early 15th-century works which Bukofzer once described as being in 'panconsonant' style[1] can be seen the seeds of what was to become known as the suspension, as in the following example from John Dunstable (c. 1370–1453):

EX.34 John Dunstable: *Sancta Maria*

[1] Manfred Bukofzer, *Studies in Medieval and Renaissance Music (1950)*, p.74.

Bukofzer pointed out that it was in this body of music that dissonance first became regulated, in striking contrast to its use in earlier medieval music where it arose largely as a result of the collision of independent voices. This can be seen in the following extract from an anonymous 13th-century motet where the parts, each moving with melodic purposefulness and seeming independence, often clash with apparent disregard for each other; yet the disparate elements are so compellingly brought together that they assume a relationship both complementary and dynamic.

EX.35

It will be seen that the often abrasive dissonances are, in a sense, incidental; and what is more, they tend to set each voice off from the other. In later music, dissonance (especially the suspension) provided one of the means of blending the parts.

Resolution of dissonance became characteristic of music from the 15th century to the end of the tonal era, even though the precise nature of its treatment changed from period to period. While the history of musical style from baroque times reveals a growing tolerance towards dissonance, within this general trend are also found reactions against it, as for instance in some early classical works of the mid-18th century (notably from the Mannheim School) where the harmonies are far more bland than in those of much music from the previous era. This is perhaps not surprising, for in reacting against the previous style the new one largely shed that element responsible for so many arresting passages in baroque music, i.e. counterpoint. It was when the homophonic texture was strengthened by greater contrapuntal movement in the works of Haydn and Mozart that the classical style revealed once again the poignant beauties of dissonance.

Nevertheless it seems indisputable that there has been a general trend towards increased levels of dissonance in tonal music, many of the rich chordal structures which had come into being through the interplay of voices being eventually treated as harmonic entities. The dominant 7th is a classic case. During the 17th century the seventh of this chord no longer required preparation as a suspension or treatment as a passing-note as had been customary in the previous century. Nevertheless it still required resolution as was to be the case with almost all dissonant notes. In the practice of resolution may be seen the essentially linear nature of dissonance in tonal music.

Towards the end of the 19th century dissonance underwent new developments. On the one hand it continued to follow linear practice, but totally unhampered by the restrictions of tonality. Its most striking manifestation was in the atonal and serial music of Schoenberg and his school. On the other its linear element became absorbed into chordal entities (as had been the case with the dominant 7th), particularly at first in the music of Debussy who, by also breaking away from the traditional syntax of chord progression, opened the way for the concept of dissonance as sonority or density. The most striking recent manifestation of this tendency has been in the field of electronic music.

While the 20th century has witnessed an unprecedented level of music experimentation, it has also seen an unprecedented interest in music of the past. Those with open and receptive minds seem to adjust intuitively to the many styles of European music, even to those of the more remote periods. As far as dissonance is concerned, no matter how accustomed our ears have become to a range of sounds unheard before our century, and many of them strident in the extreme, we are still able to respond keenly to the milder harmonies of earlier tonal music. The abrasiveness of a Bartók string quartet in no way blunts our sensitivity to the subtle eloquence of Mozart's language in the same medium. It is a question of context; a study of some of the principles of dissonance at work in tonal music can only increase this sensitivity towards one of its most expressive elements.

Dissonances may be conveniently classified in the following categories:

1 Unaccented Passing Notes
2 Unaccented Auxiliary Notes
3 Unaccented dissonances approached by leap
4 Unaccented dissonances quitted by leap of a 3rd in opposite direction
5 Anticipations
6 Appoggiaturas approached by leap
7 Appoggiaturas approached by step (accented Passing and Auxiliary Notes)
8 Suspensions

In our analyses ornamental resolutions are shown by an arrow.

Unaccented Dissonances
It is useful to distinguish between two kinds of dissonance practice. One is where, either through speed or lack of emphasis, the harmonic clash is barely perceptible, as in these opening bars of Bach's Two-Part Invention in F:

EX.36 J. S. Bach: *Invention in F*

F: I

Here the notes foreign to the chord of F major (prevailing over the three bars) act as links between the more emphatic notes of the arpeggio. They are usually called unaccented *passing notes,* and in this example most of them receive little or no accents. In our list of dissonances they comprise Category 1.

As well as demonstrating the technique of passing notes the passage also illustrates a fundamental principle in all regulated dissonance treatment of the period: while consonant notes (in this case those of the arpeggio) are free to leap or move in any way, dissonant notes have restricted movement. Their goal or resolution is to the note immediately above or below. Usually this goal is attained on the next move, but composers (notably Bach) have also exploited the possibilities of briefly postponing the goal in a technique called ornamental resolution (see p.57).

A further point illustrated by the passage is that in tonal harmony the concept of dissonance is not so much an interval clash (e.g. 2nds and 7ths sounding together) as a conflict between the prevailing *chord* and a note foreign to it. Thus, in the second bar of Bach's Invention, the D in the right hand is not dissonant with the F in the left hand (it is a major 6th) but with the implied chord of F major. It is this *harmonic* consideration which partly distinguishes dissonance practice in tonal music from that found in renaissance music which, on the other hand, was more restricted in other ways.

A variant of the passing-note technique is where the dissonance is resolved by returning to the consonant note sounded immediately before it, as in this figure from Bach's *Goldberg Variations* where both the 'upper' and 'lower' forms of the so-called *auxiliary notes* are used (Category 2):

EX.37 J. S. Bach: *Goldberg Variations*

The next figure in the same bar brings us closer to the other main group of dissonances: those which draw attention to themselves, and which are therefore exploited particularly for their expressive character.

EX.38 Ibid

Although the F♯ in the melody is not on the beat and is therefore an unaccented note it is thrown into greater prominence by the leap from B. This is intensified later in the piece when the opening motif is expanded by upward leaps to the dissonance:

EX.39 Ibid

Because those dissonances which fall on normally unaccented notes achieve a degree of emphasis when approached by a leap, it often becomes difficult to classify them as 'accented' or 'unaccented', and of course tempo plays a critical part in the over-all effect. The dissonances illustrated at Exx.38 and 39 represent the first step towards the accented type simply because of the involvement of a leap. Figures such as these are very common, particularly in music of the baroque era. An unaccented dissonance approached by a leap will be classified as Category 3.

There is a special category of unaccented dissonance the resolution of which is achieved, not by moving to a note immediately above or below, but by the leap of a 3rd in the opposite direction. Some textbooks classify this as *échappé* (suggesting that the dissonance has 'escaped' its resolution). It was particularly popular in the 18th-century classical school where it was used as a stereotyped embellishment of a scale-passage (often in conjunction with parallel 3rds and 6ths). It will form Category 4: unaccented dissonances quitted by the leap of a 3rd in the opposite direction.

EX.40 Mozart: *Piano Sonata in B♭, K333*

Another unaccented dissonance, the *anticipation* (Category 5) needs no explanation.

EX.41 Beethoven: *Sonata in G, Op. 49, No. 2*

Accented Dissonances

We turn next to the second main grouping of dissonances: those which fall on an accent. It has already been pointed out that the matter of stress or emphasis is not necessarily clear-cut, for there are many factors which affect this. The leap to a dissonance on a metrically unaccented note is a case in point. But when leap and metrical accent coincide the dissonance carries with it a poignancy much exploited by composers throughout the tonal period, as illustrated in these examples of the so-called *appoggiatura* or 'leaning note' (Category 6).

EX.42 (a) Mozart: *String Quartet, K456*

(b) Saint-Saëns: *Samson et Dalila*

The 'leaning' effect of the appoggiatura is also conveyed in passages where the leap of the dissonance is absent, stress arising from the metrical accent only:

EX.43 J. S. Bach: *Prelude No. 7, 48 Preludes and Fugues, Book I*

It will be seen from Ex.43 that such appoggiaturas are the same as what many textbooks describe as 'accented passing notes'. There is no need to quibble over this terminology, but it is worth recalling how the notation of many an 18th-century score (as Ex.44) reveals the true appoggiatura character of this kind of dissonance treatment (Category 7). Into this category we will also place accented auxiliary notes.

EX.44 Mozart: *Twelve Variations, K353*

Suspensions
Ex.43 also illustrates the use of the other important stressed dissonance, the *suspension*. At the third crotchet beat, D is sounded as the 7th of a dominant 7th chord built on E♭. When the rest of the chord moves to the triad of A♭ (2nd inversion) the D♭ remains suspended for a moment before dropping to C. At the moment of suspension a dissonance is produced on a metrically stressed part of the bar.

This sequence of events is usually described as 'preparation' (sounding a note as part of a chord), 'suspension' (holding or repeating this note so that its delayed movement causes it to become foreign to the prevailing chord at an emphatic moment) and 'resolution' (moving the note by step to its original, but delayed goal). As the following examples show, the suspension is prepared on a weak beat, sounded on a strong beat and resolved on a weak one. These principles underlie all suspension treatment during the tonal period no matter how varied the texture and style (Category 8).

EX.45

(a) D. Scarlatti: *Sonata in C minor, K158*

(b) Chorale: *O Haupt voll Blut und Wunden* (harm. J. S. Bach)

(c) Schubert: *Du bist die Ruh*

(d) J. S. Bach: *Prelude No. 1, 48 Preludes and Fugues, Book I*

Suspension treatment will form Category 8

Ornamental Resolution
Mention was made earlier of the technique often known as 'ornamental resolution'. Here the dissonant note delays its resolution by first moving to another note or group of notes. The most frequently encountered type is that where the dissonant note leaps a 3rd (upwards or downwards) before reaching its true goal. An example of this can be seen at the beginning of Ex.44, where the F♯ of the grace-notes moves a diminished 3rd upwards before resolving to G. Another example by the same composer exploits the same kind of ornamental resolution very beautifully.

EX.46 Mozart: *Sonata in F, K533*

Sometimes the resolution may be considerably delayed, as in the following two examples from Bach. The second is particularly striking in that the eventual resolution takes place in a register lower than that in which the dissonance is sounded.

EX.47 (a) J. S. Bach: *Prelude No. 12, 48 Preludes and Fugues, Book I*

(b) J. S. Bach: *Partita No. 1*

We will not place ornamental resolutions in a specific category, for obviously they occur *after* a dissonance. In the assignments for this chapter, they will however be identified by an arrow.

Other dissonance treatment
Before leaving the question of resolution, mention must be made of a practice sometimes employed with the dominant 13th:

EX.48

C: V^{13}

The most usual resolution of this note is a step downwards before the dominant chord moves to the tonic. In a practice sometimes known as an 'elliptical resolution' the note moves directly to the tonic as in this example:

EX.49 Chopin: *Ballade No. 1*

The imposition of a dominant chord (usually a dominant 7th) over a tonic note is a dissonance so frequently found at cadences that it must be accounted for in our list of common practices. It can be interpreted either as a chordal appoggiatura to the tonic or a multiple dissonance over it.

EX.50 (a) Beethoven: *Piano Sonata in C minor, Op. 10, No. 1*

(b) Mozart: *Piano Sonata in D, K311*

Dissonance may also be achieved by sustaining a note (or notes) throughout changing harmonies, a technique called pedal-point. Its function is three-fold: to generate greater tension in familiar vocabulary, to give a compelling sense of unity to chordal progressions and to hold back the onward thrust of the harmony. (When analysing such passages it is customary to write the symbols without accounting for the sustained note unless it forms part of a recognized chordal structure.)

EX.51 Beethoven: *Piano Sonata in F, Op. 54*

So far our study of dissonance has seen it as a vertical phenomenon, i.e. dissonance is produced by sounding *together* a chord and a note or group of notes foreign to it. Yet there is also a powerful form of dissonance known as 'false relations', the impact of which comes not through the simultaneous sounding of conflicting elements but by their *immediate juxtaposition*. False relations occur when a note in one voice is chromatically altered in *another* voice, their juxtaposition producing a harmonic dislocation. Some false relations are barely noticeable, others may be quite striking. While traditional textbooks warn students against producing false relations in their harmony exercises, some composers have exploited the effect, as did Mozart in his String Quartet in C, K465, appropriately nicknamed 'The Dissonant'.

EX.52 Mozart: *String Quartet in C, K465*

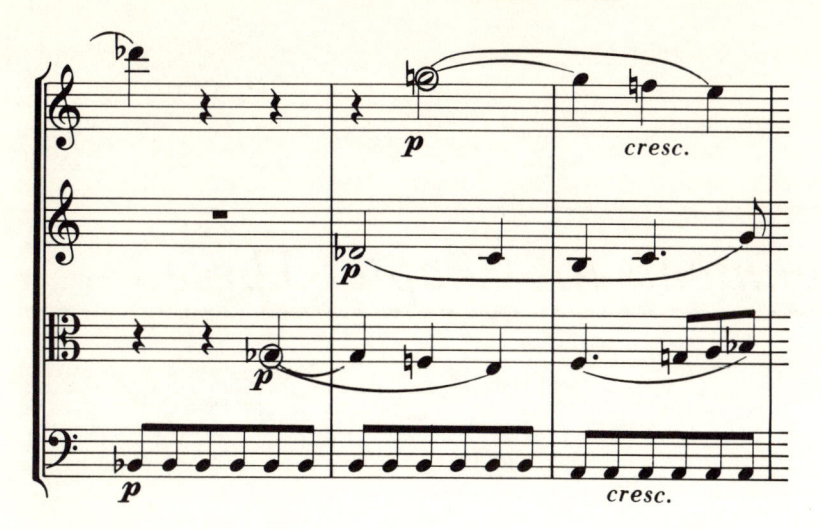

We have now examined the most frequently used dissonance techniques and have seen that while some pass over the dissonance very lightly, others highlight it. All of them (except those achieved by 'juxtaposition') are regulated by the principle of stepwise resolution even though this may be briefly postponed. Through the anticipation of resolution which dissonance arouses in our conditioned response to the style, tonal harmony seems to gain a sense of onward movement, and of course in partnership with other elements helps generate sensations of tension and relaxation. Thus dissonance serves two functions: while it carries an emotional significance on many occasions, at all times is it involved in the dynamic process of 'construction'.

It would be wrong to conclude with the impression that during the 300 years which concern our study no composer deviated from the techniques outlined in this chapter. There are many passages in J. S. Bach, for example, which defy traditional usage, while Monteverdi probably went further than most of his successors in unusual treatment of dissonance. Nevertheless the principles of dissonance treatment described above created a technical norm which, while affording composers considerable scope for the exploitation of dissonance, provided for the clear articulation of those chord progressions which formed the basic syntax of tonal harmony.

Assignments for Chapter Three

1 Using the various categories of dissonance discussed so far in Chapter Three, add an upper part to the following bass lines. Maintain the continuous flow of semiquavers as shown at the beginning, avoiding immediate note-repetition as this tends to hold up the melodic flow. Circle each note dissonant with the prevailing chord and observe the restrictions placed upon its movement according whatever category of dissonances is under consideration. You will need to take care over consecutives. Aim to produce a shapely melody that also sounds well with the bass.

(a) Illustrating use of Categories 1 and 2

G: Ia   Ib   IVa IVb Va Vb   I   via vib iia iib V   I

(b) Illustrating use of Categories 1, 2 and 3

(same harmonies)

(c) Including examples of Categories 6 and 7

(same harmonies)

(d) Recast the melody line of the following to introduce suspensions at each asterisk. Ensure that each suspension follows the pattern of preparation, suspension and resolution, and then indicate the intervals involved as shown below.

G: I   iib   V   vi   Ib   ii   V⁷   I

Continue as follows:

(3   7   6)

64 DISSONANCE

2 Identify the dissonances found in these two pieces by Bach. For the present purpose, regard each crotchet as an accented beat in the first piece (a), and each quaver as an accented note in the second piece (b).

(a) **Menuet**

B♭: I   ii V I ii   V⁷ I

V⁷   I V I IV V I   V

(b) **Fantasia**

a: i   V⁷   i   V⁷

i   V⁹₇   a: {VIb / C: {IVb   V⁷

I   vi   ii   V   I   IV   V

3 (a)   Identify the dissonances in these opening bars of Chopin's *Berceuse*. (The entire work is based upon tonic/dominant harmonies.)

(b) Compose a continuation of this work for at least eight bars. Except in arpeggio figures the leading-note and sub-dominant should resolve to tonic and mediant respectively when harmonized by the dominant 7th chord.

4 Musical practice during the baroque period included the 'gracing' of slow movements, i.e. dissolving the longer notes of the melody into decorative figures.[1] Such figures embraced all the dissonance-types discussed in this chapter, especially passing notes. Following the style suggested below, 'grace' this extract from a sonata for recorder and continuo by Telemann.

---

[1] For information about this practice, see Robert Donington, *Baroque Music: Style and Performance* (Faber, 1982), or other standard references.

5   This assignment is based upon Brahms' Intermezzo in E major. At first sight it appears to have a chordal texture. Yet it is essentially contrapuntal because of the presence of so many dissonances which must resolve, and in so doing create interweaving 'lines' which decorate the harmony. The following steps will help clarify the point:

(i) Write out the basic harmonies of the Intermezzo as indicated by the symbols placed underneath the left-hand part, retaining Brahms' chord spacing as shown:

(ii) Using these as a reference, circle each dissonant note in Brahms' piece, identify the category of dissonance and trace the resolution.

(iii) Sing the lines which have been created through these resolutions, trying to develop sensitivity to the way the notes move in response to the tonal forces set up by Brahms' harmonies. Can you explain the subtle change in texture after the pause?

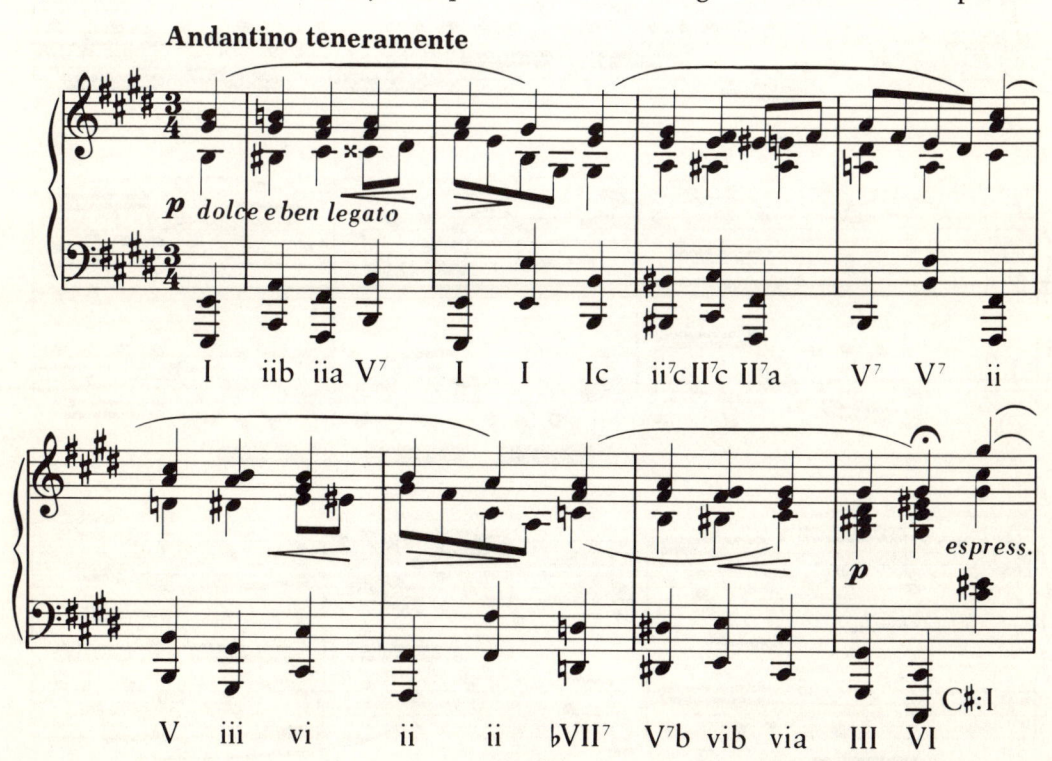

6   Analyse the harmonic structure of the following extract. Place a circle around each dissonant note and do not take them into account in your analysis.

Beethoven: *Piano Sonata in E♭, Op. 7*

DISSONANCE

CHAPTER FOUR
CHROMATICISM AND MODULATION

CHROMATICISM

In dealing with chromaticism the present chapter is largely concerned with basic principles. If we first grasp the broad concept of chromaticism in tonal harmony, we are then in a better position to study the details of its usage, and to realize that behind the apparent diversity of chromatic vocabulary (set out in the next chapter) there lies a remarkable affinity. While chromaticism often makes its appearance in the form of melodic decoration – and thus follows the principles of dissonance treatment outlined in Chapter Three – it may also be absorbed into the harmony, forming chords which have become recognizable units of tonal syntax. It is this latter kind of chromaticism with which we are concerned.

We have seen in Chapter One how the modal system was modified by the introduction of notes orginally foreign to it, a process which was to lead to the emergence of major and minor scales and the eventual concept of tonality. It was during the second half of the 16th century, especially in the passionate Italian madrigal, that the use of chromatic notes increased markedly. At first sight this might seem to suggest a hastening towards tonality; but in fact there are many chromatic passages in very late renaissance music which have little 'tonal' feel about them, as in this extract from Gesualdo's madrigal *Tu piango filli mia*:

EX.53 Gesualdo: *Tu piango filli mia*

Compare this with a piece of Bach which has a chromatic descending melody superficially similar to the lines in Gesualdo's piece.

EX.54 J. S. Bach: *Musical Offering*

There is clearly a world of difference between this tonally-directed chromaticism and that which is sometimes found in music which was written before the tonal period. Nevertheless there are also many chromatic passages in renaissance music which do indeed foreshadow those in baroque to romantic music, as in the following example, an extract from Luzzaschi's famous *Quivi sospiri* composed some 35 years before Gesualdo's *Tu piango filli mia*:

EX.55 Luzzaschi: *Quivi sospiri*

What are the threads which connect the pieces by Luzzaschi and Bach, and yet which by-pass that by Gesualdo?

The first connection is the way in which the chromaticism in Luzzaschi and Bach has become involved in dominant-type progressions, i.e. progressions in which one chord is preceded by a major chord whose root is a perfect 4th below that of the next. Thus, in the Luzzaschi extract the first triad (B♭, 1st inversion) moves to one built on root E♭. The first triad could be said to have a dominant relationship to the second (even though it is not on the dominant degree of the scale or mode). In the following analysis note how the chromaticism produces 'leading-note' functions in some of the triads.

EX.56

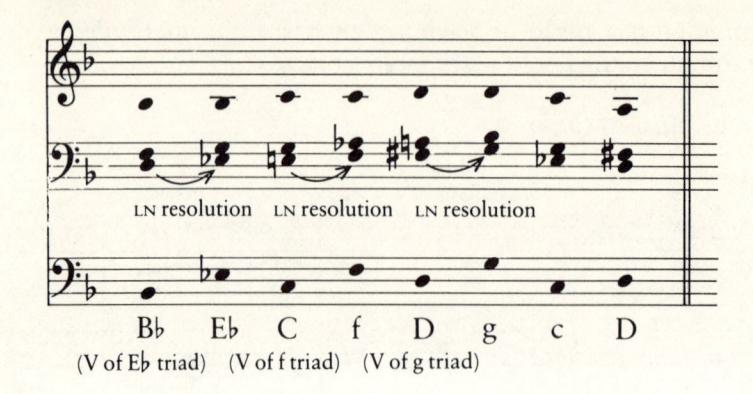

[musical example with annotations: LN resolution, LN resolution, LN resolution; Bb Eb C f D g c D; (V of Eb triad) (V of f triad) (V of g triad)]

In Bach's piece the chromaticism heightens still further the dominant-type progressions by producing chords identical to dominant 7ths. It will be noted in the analysis below that the root movement is an uninterrupted Cycle of 5ths (see pp. 20-23). In this piece the chromatic 'leading-notes' in the solo part do not rise, but fall a semitone each time in accordance with the melodic pattern which Bach has designed.

EX.57

[musical example labelled "Harmonic basis", ending with *etc.*]

Thus the first point to be noted is that tonally-directed chromaticism is characteristically involved in dominant-type structures and progressions, and this tendency permeates even the richest pages in Wagner, as the following extract from *Tristan* illustrates. This music extends the principle demonstrated in the Luzzaschi and Bach extracts merely by resolving some of the chromatically produced dominant 7th chords to chords other than those with roots a fourth above, and by introducing a rich flow of dissonance in the form of chromatic passing-notes and so on. As these do not form part of the chordal structure they have been omitted from the analysis which is set out underneath Wagner's music.

EX.58 Wagner: *Prelude to Tristan und Isolde*

Langsam und schmachtend

Harmonic basis

Root movement

[Dominant 7ths marked *]

Basic to all that has been said and illustrated so far is the fact that the notes above the root of a triad may be chromatically altered and yet the *function* of the chord remains the same. Indeed, as we have seen, the relationship of one chord to another may become even stronger through chromatic alteration, as for example when the 3rd of a minor triad becomes major and acts as a kind of 'leading-note'. So, in the supertonic to dominant progression II – V is more compelling than ii – V:

EX.59

ii V II V

If the 5th of a major triad is chromatically raised the expectations of its resolution are even stronger, as Beethoven shows in the Scherzo movement of his 'Pastoral' Sonata.

EX.60 Beethoven: *Piano Sonata in D, Op. 28*

To illustrate this basic principle of chromaticism changing the 'colour' of a chord without altering its function, let us return to the Luzzaschi extract and inflect the notes of each triad differently, major 3rds becoming minor 3rds, etc. Aurally compare the original (Ex.55) with the following:

EX.61

It will be noticed that the chords retain their original relationship, the only change being the different 'colourings' of major and minor.

One of the most striking examples of the same principle is seen at work in Chopin's E minor Prelude. Here the throbbing left-hand chords subtly change hue as one note after another drops by step in the expression of profound grief. Yet despite the richness of sonority and the eloquence of voice-leading, the harmonic basis of the first four bars, for example, is simply i V I, each chord suspended in time as it were while its notes are chromatically altered one by one.

EX.62 Chopin: *Prelude in E minor*

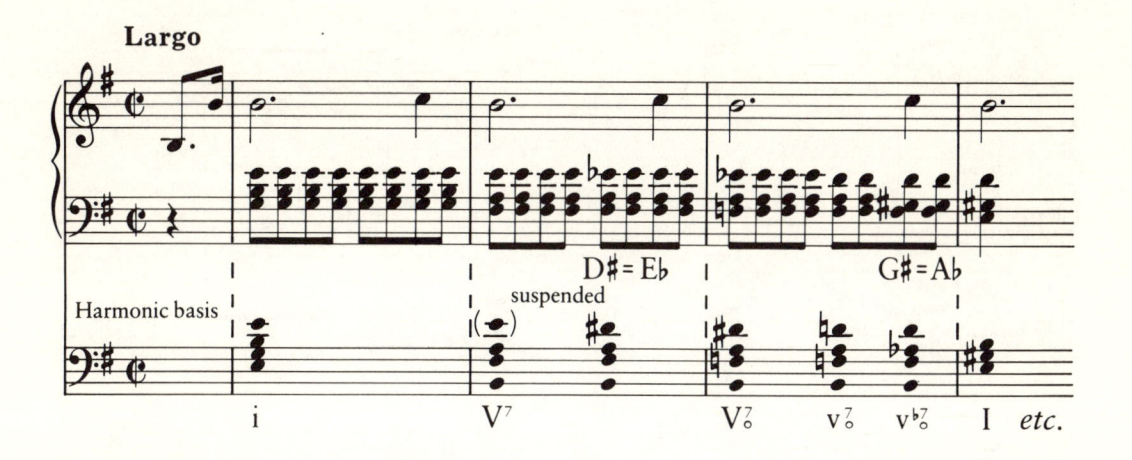

It will be seen that the analysis becomes clear by recognizing certain enharmonic equivalents (e.g. D♯/E♭). This is symptomatic of the problems imposed on notation when 19th century composers began exploring the last reaches of tonality. The subtleties of the harmonic system often went beyond what the notes could show, a point that will become clearer in the next chapter. What needs to be grasped at this point, however, is the fact that Chopin's miraculous piece was in a sense made possible only because of the properties of chromaticism discussed in this chapter.

All that has been said so far is just another way of putting the idea that tonal chromaticism grows out of the diatonic syntactical processes. As Nadia Boulanger was fond of saying: chromaticism is implied in diatonicism. It is this which sets the Luzzaschi and Bach pieces apart from that by Gesualdo. His chordal progressions in Ex.53, strikingly beautiful as they are, are not those which help generate the kind of tonality characteristic of music written from the 17th century to the 19th century. Far from strengthening the basic tonal relationships, his chromaticism in this piece has loosened them: B major, B minor, F minor, C major, B♭ major, A minor, F♯ major.

A parallel can be drawn between tonal chromaticism and the principles of dissonance treatment discussed in the previous chapter. Both provided composers with elements which could be fully exploited while still retaining the clear articulation of tonal syntax. Like dissonance, chromaticism is essentially a linear phenomenon, sometimes absorbed into the chordal structure, sometimes standing in relief to it when chromaticism and dissonance become identical. Both chromaticism and dissonance helped expand classical syntax, so that in the 19th century those pillars of clear tonality (ii V i, and other formulae) were often separated by profuse 'decorative' harmony in which chromaticism played such an important part. Yet even in extravagantly chromatic passages it is usually possible to perceive the basic diatonic processes, as in this phrase from the poignant theme of César Franck's *Variations Symphoniques:*

EX.63 Franck: *Variations Symphoniques*

This piece, like Chopin's Prelude and Wagner's *Tristan* is merely an extension of the same principles seen in Luzzaschi and Bach. When writers talk of *Tristan* containing the seeds of atonality this can only be justified in terms of the constantly fluctuating key-centres — a point that brings us immediately to a consideration of modulation.

Modulation
At first sight the term 'modulation' might seem to be related to mode and modal music. But in fact its derivation is not from *modus* but *modulari* (to adjust), and it occurs principally in tonal music. This is not to deny that its germ may be found in those cadences brought about by musica ficta (see p.13) in modal pieces, but in these cases the effect is that of emphasizing certain *degrees* of the mode rather than a shift to a new mode. As we shall see there are certain tonal parallels in this, but, as the main concern of modulation is to bring about shifts of key-centre (and this is in itself a complex matter), it is better for us to examine the processes in their fully developed, rather than evolutionary, stage.

Superficially the idea of modulation or key change is very simple; in the actual practice of art-music it may not be so easily defined or clear-cut. This is because it comprises a complex of factors that no rule-of-thumb can measure, for in each case the relationships of these factors are changed — sometimes only slightly — and each situation has to be judged on its own terms.

The problem is not helped at the outset by disagreement amongst theorists as to what the term modulation really means. For some it implies a very smooth, almost imperceptible movement from one key to another; for others it also includes abrupt changes. And while some textbooks have encouraged one to regard every dominant 7th chord foreign to the main key as indicating a modulation (often called a *transition* in this context), there are also theorists who reject conventional ideas about modulation to such an extent that a piece of music might be regarded as being in one key throughout. This latter approach is often associated with analyses which attempt to abstract and compress the events of a composition (its 'foreground') in order to discover its structural and harmonic quintessence or 'background'. If such abstraction takes one's understanding of a composition to an intellectual level removed from the immediate aural experience, this does not mean that the other extreme just mentioned is any closer.

To understand what factors are involved in the phenomenon of modulation let us begin by examining Bach's setting of the chorale *Wer nur den lieben Gott lässt walten*. Its opening and closing phrases are very clearly in the key of B minor, whereas the middle phrases both contain progressions associated with D major. Play the chorale several times to discover why the third phrase gives a stronger impression of D major than does the preceding one.

EX.64 Chorale: *Wer nur den lieben Gott lässt walten* (harm. J. S. Bach)

Clearly there are two main factors at work. The first is that all-important aspect of musical form: time-span. In the second phrase the V – I progression in D has scarcely time to make its impact before B minor is re-asserted, while in the third phrase the D major progressions are given a span of six beats. (This of course must be related to another time-span, that of the chorale as a whole; in a longer, faster work six beats may be negligible.) The other main factor concerns the positioning of V – I. In one phrase it is touched upon only in passing – in the middle of that phrase – while in the other the progression is not only repeated but achieves aural prominence by being placed at a cadence point. As a result of both these factors the key of D is more strongly asserted in the third phrase. Yet even at this point there would be those who regard the third phrase as highlighting III of B minor rather than I of D major. Now the question of modulation enters the realm of individual differences in aural response, especially in the capacity to retain a sense of key-centre. For example, a modulation to the dominant, strengthened by time-span and emphatic placement, may still give the impression to some listeners that the music is on the dominant rather than in it. It is probably this factor more than any other which has caused so many conflicting views on modulation, in particular about the so-called 'pivot-chord'.

In essence the pivot-chord marks simultaneously the 'end' of one key and the 'beginning' of the next, i.e. it is approached in one key and left in another, and hence is common to both. Thus in the third phrase of the chorale the B minor triad may be interpreted as functioning as i in B minor and vi in D major:

EX.65

The presence of pivot-chords contributes to the smooth movement from one key to the next, and the typical analysis of such a situation as shown at Ex.65 is a useful way of showing the process. The objection to it is that such an analysis does not necessarily represent the *musical* situation, for as we have seen, new keys may take time to be established and old ones may persist in the memory. How for example can any analysis indicate definitively the subtle unfolding of keys in a work such as the following?

EX.66 J. S. Bach: *French Suite in E♭*

[E♭: vib]
[B♭: iib]

Some may hear the return of the note A♭ in bar 5 (previously altered to A♯ in the dominant-tending bars) as suggesting a return to the old tonic before the new key is clinched at the cadence; others may feel that the B♭ tonality is already so firmly entrenched that the note A♭ is now like a *chromatic* flattened 7th alteration. The most any analysis can indicate is the general trend. The reference to the pivot-chord in the second half of the third bar is certainly useful provided that one realizes the many factors at work in the process of modulation, not least the time-span. Once this is recognized the importance of the pivot-chord principle becomes less debatable.

The real significance of the pivot-chord is that it vividly illustrates one of the most important harmonic properties of tonality: every chord embodies a multiplicity of possible functions. Thus we saw in the chorale that the triad of B minor functioned simultaneously as i in B minor and vi in D major. These are only two of its possible functions. As there are 24 different keys each triad has *theoretically* the same number of possible functions, but in practice all these are not evident for the reason that some harmonic progressions are more convincing than others in the context of tonality. To see some of the functional possibilities latent in a single chord let us return to the Air from Bach's French Suite.

In this extract Bach has taken the C minor triad in the third bar as a means of moving smoothly into the region of B♭ major, employing it as part of the progression ii – V in that key. Yet this was only one of the possibilities, for the same triad has powerful functions also in G minor (iv) and C minor (i), keys that Bach could have touched had he so wished. The same triad has less powerful functions in other keys: F minor (v), A♭ (iii), and through the process of chromatic inflection discussed earlier in this chapter it functions chromatically in the major or minor opposites of the keys mentioned above.

The range of functions becomes even wider through the inclusion of enharmonic equivalents, some examples of which will be studied in the next chapter. But sufficient has probably been said to indicate why tonality was so rich in modulatory possibilities. The multiplicity of functions embodied in every chord is undoubtedly the major reason why tonality proved to be such an extraordinarily supple medium, providing a system which composers were to explore and exploit for nearly three centuries before exhausting its possibilities. If much of the music written in the first two centuries of its history exhibits relatively clear definitions of fairly closely related key-centres and direct means of achieving them, that of the later century explored other relationships and methods. And how well tonality yielded to the romantic temper that delighted in blurred outlines, suggestion and evocation.

It was stated earlier in this chapter that theoretically each triad embodies 24 potential functions, but in practice this is not evident because not all chordal progressions generate tonality. In a sense it could be argued that as every chord is related in some way then it becomes virtually impossible not to modulate without using a chordal nexus which could be called a pivot. However the term 'pivot-chord' has tended to be used in relation only to those chords which have a strong function with the dominant of the new key — supertonic, sub-dominant, tonic, sub-mediant and the chromatic chords of the flattened 2nd and 6th together with the augmented chords known as Italian, French and German 6ths (see pp. 98-100).

Keys which are not linked by a pivot-chord (using the more restricted terminology) may have a single note in common, or the bass line may move by step, both devices helping to achieve smoothness. On the other hand, a composer may wish to establish a new key with dramatic contrast, as does Haydn in this excerpt from the Piano Sonata in E♭.

EX.67 Haydn: *Piano Sonata in E♭ No. 52*

That modulation is one of the chief means of gaining expression is easily demonstrated, and some composers, particularly the Romantics, emphasized this element to a high degree. But like dissonance, modulation is at all times associated with musical form. Through it ideas are *expanded* with that sense of onward thrust so characteristic of tonal music. In the final chapter of this book we shall examine the interaction of modulation and structure.

Assignments for Chapter Four

1   Write out the Cycle of 5ths in the key of D minor and compare this with Fauré's treatment of the same sequence in his *Après un rêve* (Ex.22, p.22). Analyse Fauré's song by placing symbols under the bass line, taking the dissonant notes into account. Trace the resolution of these dissonant notes.

2   Harmonically analyse Schumann's song, *Die Lotosblume,* using symbols underneath the bass line. You may have to distinguish between passages that exhibit chromaticism and those which are modulatory. In some cases you may wish to show alternative analyses. Where modulations are introduced through pivot-chords show the pivot-chord in two keys,

e.g. F I
     C IV V I

Are there any modulations in this piece which do not exhibit pivot-chords? If this is the case, explain the process.

Find examples in Schumann's song which illustrate the idea that the chromatic inflection of a triad does not necessarily alter its function.

Ziemlich langsam

Die Lo - tos - blu - me äng - stigt

sich vor der Son - ne Pracht, und mit ge-senk-tem Haup - te er-war-tet sie träu-mend die Nacht. Der Mond, der ist ihr Buh - le, er-weckt sie mit sei - nem Licht, und ihm ent - schlei-ert sie freund - lich ihr from - mes Blu-men-ge-sicht. Sie

blüht und glüht und leuch - tet, und star - ret stumm in die
Höh', sie duf - tet und wei - net und zit - tert vor
rit.
Lie-be und Lie - bes-weh vor Lie-be und Lie - bes weh.
rit.
p

CHAPTER FIVE
EXTENSIONS OF THE TRIADIC FOUNDATION

Having examined the major concepts associated with tonal harmony we will now turn our attention to specific chordal constructions and their function.

Secondary 7ths
It has been emphasized that the chordal structures we have been examining so far should be interpreted as the outcome of linear movement the direction of which in tonal music is influenced by that syntax which gives the style its special character. This is most clearly seen in chords which include a dissonant element, such as the following:

EX.68 Chorale: *Für Freuden lasst uns springen* (harm. J. S. Bach)

Here, through suspensions, are formed two versions of the chord of the supertonic 7th:

EX.69

It comprises a minor 3rd, perfect 5th and minor 7th from the root. Like all chords of the 7th with an intervallic structure different from the dominant 7th, this one is known as a secondary 7th. Here are all the secondary 7ths in the keys of C major and C minor, the latter having of course greater variety because of the instability of the sub-mediant and leading-note in the minor key. Analyse the intervallic structure of each chord.

EX.70

(a) C: I⁷ ii⁷ iii⁷ IV⁷ vi⁷ vii⌀⁷

(b) c: i♭⁷ i⁷ ii⌀⁷ ii⁷ III⁷ III⁺⁷ iv⁷ IV⁷ VI⁷ ♯vi⌀⁷ ♭VII♭⁷ ♭VII⁷ vii⌀⁷

Ex.71 illustrates the fairly circumscribed treatment of secondary 7ths evident up to the 19th century, in that the dissonant note was always prepared and resolved (usually downwards), a train of events which can be most effectively extended throughout a Cycle of 5ths. It is a typical example. Examine each chord closely, circling each dissonant note (i.e. the 7th), to see the process unfolding in detail.

EX.71 Mozart: *Piano Sonata in F, K332*

Allegro

C: I   V⁷   i   V⁷   i

iv⁷   ♭VII♭⁷   III⁷   VI⁷   ii⁷   V⁷

The sonorous beauty of the secondary 7th was exploited particularly during the 19th century, Beethoven being one of the first seemingly to revel in its sound.

EX.72 Beethoven: *Piano Sonata in E, Op. 109*

Beethoven commences an earlier sonata by conjuring a secondary 7th out of the air, as it were. (This particular chord, the supertonic 7th in 1st inversion is known as the 'Added 6th'.) Note how some bars later he introduces other secondary 7ths, moving to the dissonances by step rather than preparing them.

EX.73 (a) Beethoven: *Piano Sonata in E♭, Op. 31, No. 3*

(b) Ibid.

Later romantic composers were to exploit fully all the emotional connotations of the secondary 7ths, especially through recourse to chromatic inflection, as shown in the next example.

EX.74 Schumann: *Ich grolle nicht*

[Musical example: Nicht zu schnell — "Ich gro-lle nicht und wenn das Herz auch bricht"]

C: I IVb IVa ii⁷₀ V⁷ I

The Diminished 7th

The chord of the diminished 7th comprises two tritones:

EX.75

These give to the various forms of the chord a restlessness and tension much exploited by romantic composers, as for example in this section of a well-known étude by Chopin.

EX.76 Chopin: *Étude, Op. 10, No. 3*

Lento ma non troppo

con bravura

The structure of the diminished 7th is different from all those so far studied in this course: a four-note chord comprising pairs of equidistant intervals (or their enharmonic equivalents):

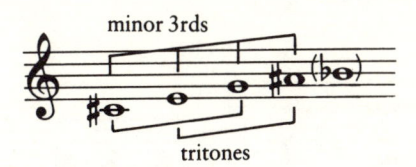

EX.77

As a result of this equal distribution of intervals the chord *as such* has no root or inversions, as the ear will quickly confirm if Ex.77 is played in different positions (starting with C♯ as the bass, then E, and so on). Nor does it seem to suggest any particular key, and hence, freed from the gravitational pull of a tonal centre, the diminished 7th gives the impression of floating in space. Its tension is generated through the conflicting tritones rather than any need to resolve. This is particularly true in extended passages, such as at Ex.76, where different diminished 7ths follow each other. (It will have been seen that there are only three different diminished 7ths, any others merely extending these three (see Ex.75). This fact is sometimes disguised, however, by different enharmonic 'spellings' of the notes, an instance of which has already been given in Ex.77.) While 19th-century composers seized upon the diminished 7th for its colour, intensity, its power to generate excitement or evoke mystery through the momentary blurring of key, earlier generations had used it in a way which, while retaining its intensity, was very closely related to traditional tonal syntax (a usage also retained by the romantics).

One of the ways in which the diminished 7th gains tonal direction is when it is used as an appoggiatura-type chord decorating a passage of conventional progressions. The tonal forces generated by such progressions urge the notes to resolve, as in this extract from a song already quoted at Ex.74.

EX.78 Schumann: *Ich grolle nicht*

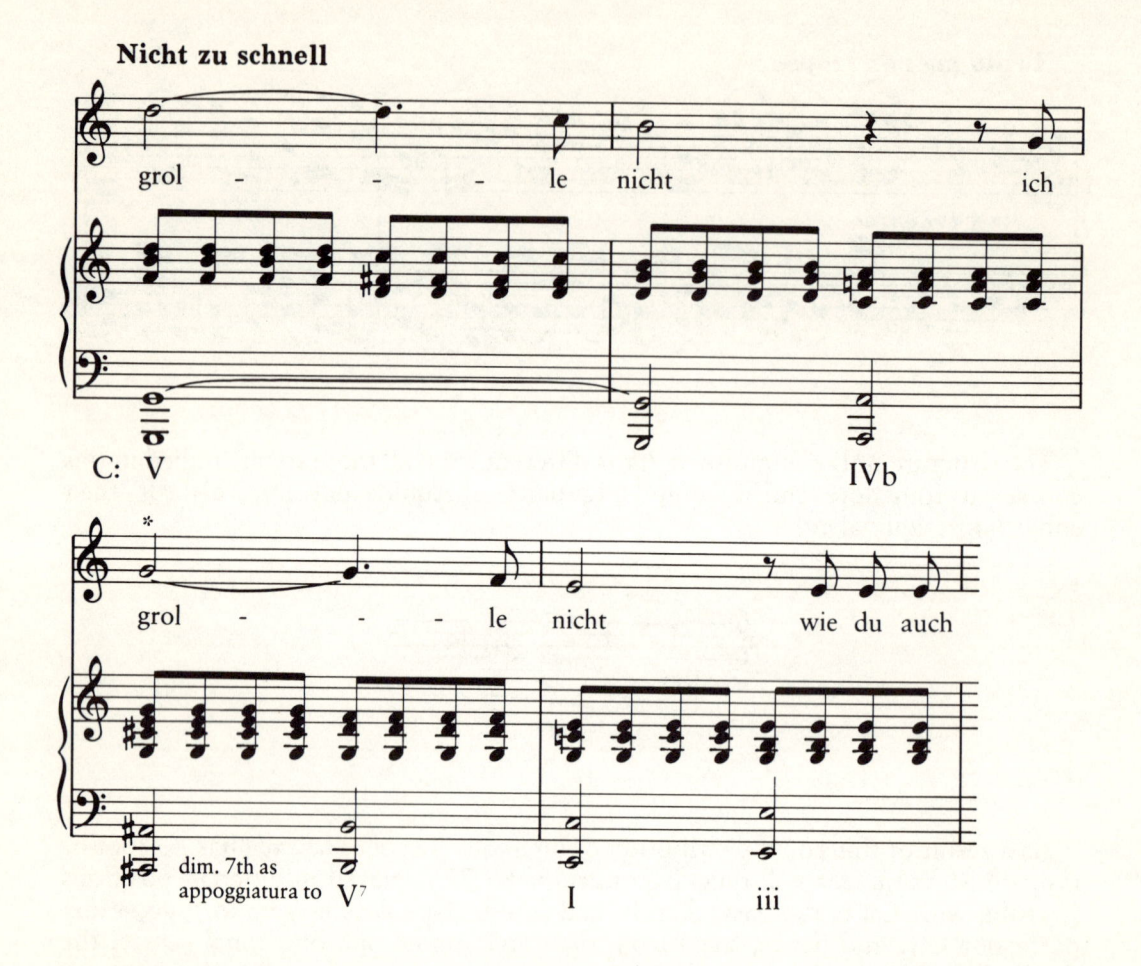

Nicht zu schnell

grol - - le nicht   ich
C: V   IVb

grol - - le nicht   wie du auch
dim. 7th as
appoggiatura to V⁷   I   iii

But it is another usage of the diminished 7th that concerns us most of all. This, the most common, is closely related to key definition.

We have seen how the chord of the diminished 5th on the leading-note may function as a dominant 7th with missing root (pp. 16-17), the force of the tritone urging its resolution this way in certain contexts. So too may the diminished 7th function like a dominant chord. Consider the following:

EX.79

C: V⁷   I   V⁷b   I   I♭⁹₇   I   V♭⁹₇b   I
            dim. 5th   dim. 7th

Despite their differing sonorities and tensions the first chords of each pair function in the same way: in the case of the diminished 7th like a dominant minor 9th with missing root. The dominant minor 9th is diatonic in a minor key and chromatic in a major one. (The same is true of the diminished 7th.) Beethoven furnishes an example of the dominant minor 9th in a major key:

EX.80 Beethoven: *Piano Sonata in F minor, Op. 2, No. 1*

Ab: V   V^{b9} I   etc.

Compare this with the diminished 7th in this extract from a later sonata:

EX.81 Beethoven: *Piano Sonata in A♭, Op. 26*

Ab: dim. 7th
                              V^{b9}b I
                              (missing root E♭)

Here are two examples which clearly illustrate how the diminished 7th may function as a dominant minor 9th with missing root:

EX.82 (a) Beethoven: *Piano Sonata in E♭, Op. 7*

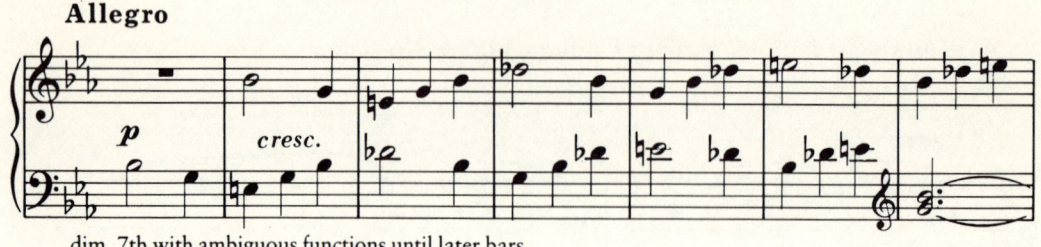

dim. 7th with ambiguous functions until later bars

f: V⁹c   ib   V⁹c   ib

(b) Schumann: *Carnaval*

c: V⁹d   ib   V⁹c   i

So far we have seen how the diminished 7th may swing free of tonal forces (as at Ex.77) or may become particularly susceptible to them when functioning as a dominant-type chord with missing root: on the one hand, ambiguity; on the other, clear definition, both of these characteristics depending entirely upon context. Thus the peculiar property of the diminished 7th is that *by itself*, it is vague and equivocal; yet it has *latent* tonal functions. To see how composers exploited this property for the purpose of modulation we will examine some bars of Beethoven's Pathétique Sonata.

EX.83 Beethoven: *Piano Sonata in C minor, Op. 13*

[musical score: Grave]

Here Beethoven first uses the diminished 7th to establish the key of G minor, and then using what appears to be the *same* chord (with different 'spelling', E♭ becoming D♯) establishes the key of E minor! In doing so he is exploiting two of the latent tonal functions of this diminished 7th, thus:

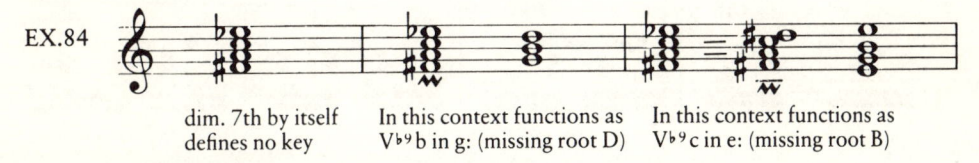

EX.84

[musical example]

dim. 7th by itself   In this context functions as   In this context functions as
defines no key   V♭9 b in g: (missing root D)   V♭9 c in e: (missing root B)

The same chord has two further functions:

EX.85

[musical example]

D♭:   V♭9 d   Ib   [NOTE: minor key version (c♯ minor)]   B♭: V♭9 e   Ic

Thus each diminished 7th chord has four latent tonal functions, each of its notes acting as four possible minor 9ths from the missing root of a dominant chord. By finding the eight missing roots, you should now be able to work out the eight possible dominant functions of the remaining two diminished 7ths.

EX. 86

(E.g., if note G of the first chord were regarded as a minor 9th above a root, that root would have to be F♯ which, acting as a dominant, would define the key as B major or minor. In this exercise it is essential to observe the correct notational spelling of each chord, this depending upon the prevailing key.)

It remains to examine a remarkable passage from Beethoven where the properties of the diminished 7th as described above are used to effect a series of breathtaking modulations.

EX. 87 Beethoven: *Piano Sonata in A, Op. 2, No. 2*

Allegro vivace

e: V⁹b   i

D♯ = E♭

V⁷c   V⁹c   G: V♭⁹b   V⁷b   I

F♯ = G♭

V⁷c   V♭⁹c   B♭: V♭⁹c   V⁷   I

V⁷c   dim. 7th used   D: V⁷b   I   I♭⁷   E: V♭⁹b   V⁷b
        as appoggiatura

$$\text{I} \quad \text{I}^{\flat 7} \quad \text{f\#: V}^9\text{b} \quad \text{V}^7\text{b} \quad \text{i}$$

The keys which Beethoven has touched in this sequential passage have been shown as modulations in order to demonstrate the dominant function of the various diminished 7ths, even though these keys have not necessarily been firmly established.

Chromatic or Secondary Dominant-Types
Compare the following harmonizations of a phrase from the chorale *Für Freuden lasst uns springen*.

EX.88 Chorale: *Für Freuden lasst uns springen*

The second (by Bach) is clearly a more sophisticated harmonization, yet making use of one of the most common forms of chromatic harmony: the secondary or chromatic dominant-type formations.

Chapter Four described how the process of chromatic inflection may alter the 'colour' of a chord without changing its function. Indeed, as we saw, chromaticism may strengthen that function. It is this principle that underlies the secondary or chromatic dominant-types (from now on to be called simply chromatic dominants).

Thus all diatonic (secondary) 7ths can be inflected to produce the dominant 7th structure of major 3rd, perfect 5th and minor 7th from the root:

EX.89

C: I^7 I$^{♭7}$ ii^7 II^7 iii^7 III^7 IV^7 IV$^{♭7}$ vi^7 VI^7 vii   VII^7

c: i^7 I^7 ii$^7_ø$ II^7 III^7 III$^{♭7}$ iv^7 IV^7 VI^7 VI$^{♭7}$ vii$^7_ø$ ♭VII$^{♭7}$

As will be expected the usual resolution of these chords is to a triad a perfect 4th above. So that our analyses will clearly indicate this dominant function, as well as the root of the chromatic chord a double set of symbols will be used (and required in all future analytical assignments). Thus:

EX.90

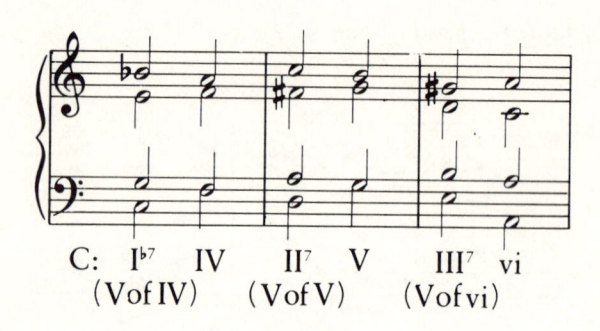

C: I$^{♭7}$ IV   II^7 V   III^7 vi
     (V of IV)   (V of V)   (V of vi)

Because ♭VII generates clear tonality only in a minor key (see Chapter One) it would be unusual to find the chromatic dominant IV$^{♭7}$ resolving to that particular chord in a major key. Indeed there are many occasions when the resolution of chromatic dominants is to a chord other than that where the root is a perfect 4th above. This is particularly evident if there is a chromatically moving bass as in Bach's harmonization above where there is a variety of resolutions. (See also the extract from *Tristan,* p.73.) In these cases there is no need to use the double set of symbols in analysis as the dominant function is not at work.

As we saw in the previous section of this chapter, diminished 7ths may also function as dominants (with missing roots) and hence be involved in the same processes as described above.

EX.91

C: I$^{♭9}_{♭7}$b   IV   II$^{♭9}$b   V   III^9 vi
     (V of IV)   (V of V)   (V of vi)

EXTENSIONS OF THE TRIADIC FOUNDATION

We are now in a position to analyse Bach's harmonization of the chorale phrase, but we will also analyse the first harmonization for the sake of comparison.

EX.92

(a)

g: i   ii V⁷c ib ii⁷b V⁷ VI   V⁹d   ib ia V

(b)

g: III   iv   IV⁷ II⁹b V   VI IV⁷b ♭VII V⁷b i   II⁹b V
                         (V of V)   (V of ♭VII)   (V of V)

The first harmonization is very obviously in the key of G minor. In the light of what has been said in Chapter Four it should also be clear that, despite the *notational* suggestions of modulation, Bach's harmonization is also in G minor throughout, none of the dominant-type chords effecting any move away from this key but merely adding colour and intensity through tonally directed chromaticism.

Chords of the Augmented 6th

Consider the following harmonizations by Bach of three chorale phrases. The chords marked * are different versions of the augmented 6th chord, the so-called Italian, French and German 6ths.

EX. 93 (a) *Ich hab' mein' Sach' Gott heimgestellt*

g:

(b) *Wer nur den lieben Gott lässt walten*

a:

(c) *Befiehl du deine Wege*

d:

Like all chromatic (as well as dissonant) chords studied so far, the augmented 6ths have their origin in contrapuntal movement, clearly demonstrated in the extracts above, although in later styles they were often treated as chordal entities. By transposing the chords as Bach used them (at Ex.93) to the key of C, their differences and similarities will become more apparent. Carefully analyse their intervallic structure.

EX.94

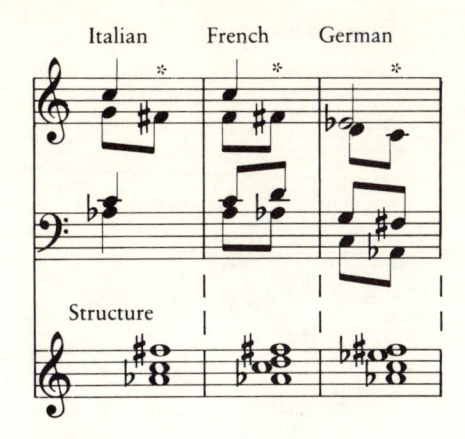

Italian   French   German

Structure

At first sight the three chords would seem to be extensions of the triad built on the flattened 6th degree of the scale (diatonic in minor keys, chromatic in major). Yet if we return to Bach's harmonizations we perceive a feature common to the three which throws a different light on these chords. In each case they resolve on to the dominant chord or its Ic decoration, and so compelling is this relationship, so clear and obvious the key definition that it prompts us to look for chord progressions which generate it. Thus we turn to the progression ii – V and see that through chromatic inflection the supertonic is the real progenitor of the augmented 6ths in this context. You should play the following transformations of the supertonic in C following every chord with the dominant so that your ear can confirm the unchanging function of the supertonic despite its chromatic inflections:

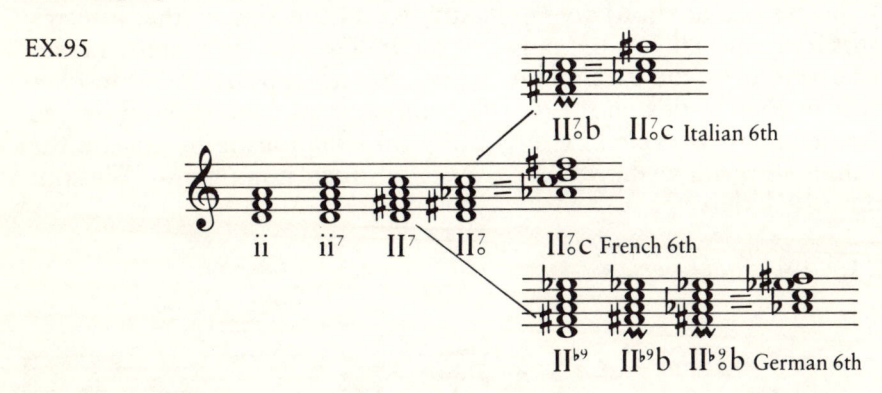

EX.95

ii   ii⁷   II⁷   II⁷∅

II⁷∅b   II⁷∅c Italian 6th

II⁷∅c French 6th

II♭⁹   II♭⁹b   II♭⁹∅b German 6th

As the process of chromatic inflection can be applied to all the diatonic chords, so there are many possibilities of augmented 6ths being used in harmony with clear tonal implications. In practice, however, they were more restricted than this would suggest. They may be found, of course, in different inversions.

Because the German 6th is the enharmonic equivalent of the dominant 7th, it is not surprising that its 'double-meaning' was effectively exploited by composers, as in this extract from Schubert's *Winterreise*:

EX.96 Schubert: *Einsamkeit (Winterreise)*

The Neapolitan 6th and other chords
Most of the chromatic chords discussed so far have been dominant-types, usually because the chromatic inflection produces a leading-note or a tritone. The final group of chords to be dealt with have no such dominant function. Prominent amongst them is the Neapolitan 6th.

Unlike the names given to the different versions of the augmented 6th, the one associated with this particular chord does at least make a little sense in that it seems to have been nurtured especially in the music of the Italian aria, although whether the chord can be traced to the Neapolitan school for its appearance is another matter. The great appeal of this chord to aria composers undoubtedly lay in the feeling of pathos it seems to evoke. Here is a typical situation in an aria by the 17th-century Italian Stradella at the words '...senza te soffrir non ponno ('Without you, cannot endure such fierce pain').

EX.97 Stradella: *Ombre, voi che celate*

From the above it will be seen that the Neapolitan 6th is a major triad built upon the flattened 2nd. Yet because it is characteristically used in 1st inversion (particularly in baroque and classical times) and so often precedes the dominant of the key, it is tempting to interpret it as iv with a chromatic appoggiatura.

But the chord was also frequently used in a sequence of 1st inversions (as in the next example), making such an interpretation difficult to sustain.

EX.98 Melani: *Vezzosa aurora*

The Neapolitan 6th gains even greater intensity when the flattened 2nd moves directly to the leading-note in the resolution to the dominant chord, the resulting melodic interval being a diminished 3rd. One of the most striking instances of this comes from Bach's B minor Mass where this curious interval permeates the whole movement of the Kyrie quoted below.

EX.99 J. S. Bach: *Kyrie* from *B minor Mass*

Because the Neapolitan 6th is so frequently associated with progressions to the dominant, it can therefore be employed before chromatic or secondary dominants, although when this does occur it is usually in music by 19th-century composers, who also occasionally use the chord in its root position. It need hardly be pointed out that its association with the dominant has provided composers with a powerful means of modulation.

In major keys the juxtaposition of a tonic triad with one a major 3rd below, i.e. a triad on the flattened sub-mediant, particularly appealed to romantic composers, although its use can be traced to music earlier than the 19th century. Here is a well-known passage from Brahms featuring this relationship:

EX.100 Brahms: *Symphony No. 3*

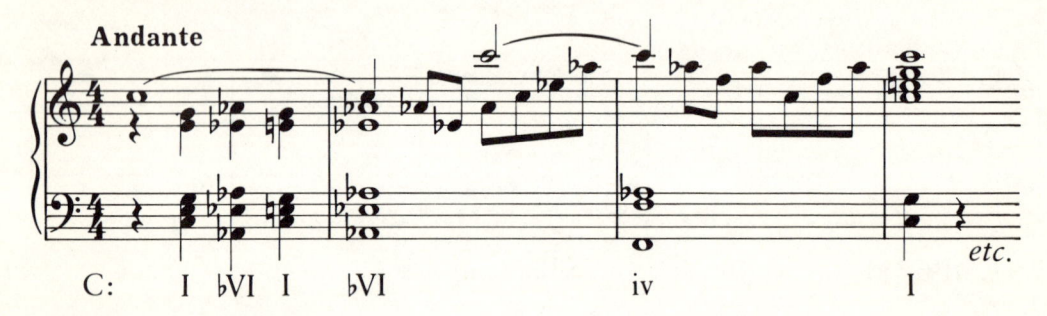

Because this chord is not dissonant it is free to resolve to any chord (in the above example, to another chromatic chord (iv)), but in practice it tends to drop a semitone to the dominant (or Ic), a progression which Hugo Wolf uses to effect a series of beautiful modulations in the following song, an analysis of which appears below it.

EX.101 (a) Wolf: *In dem Schatten meiner Locken*

(b) analysis

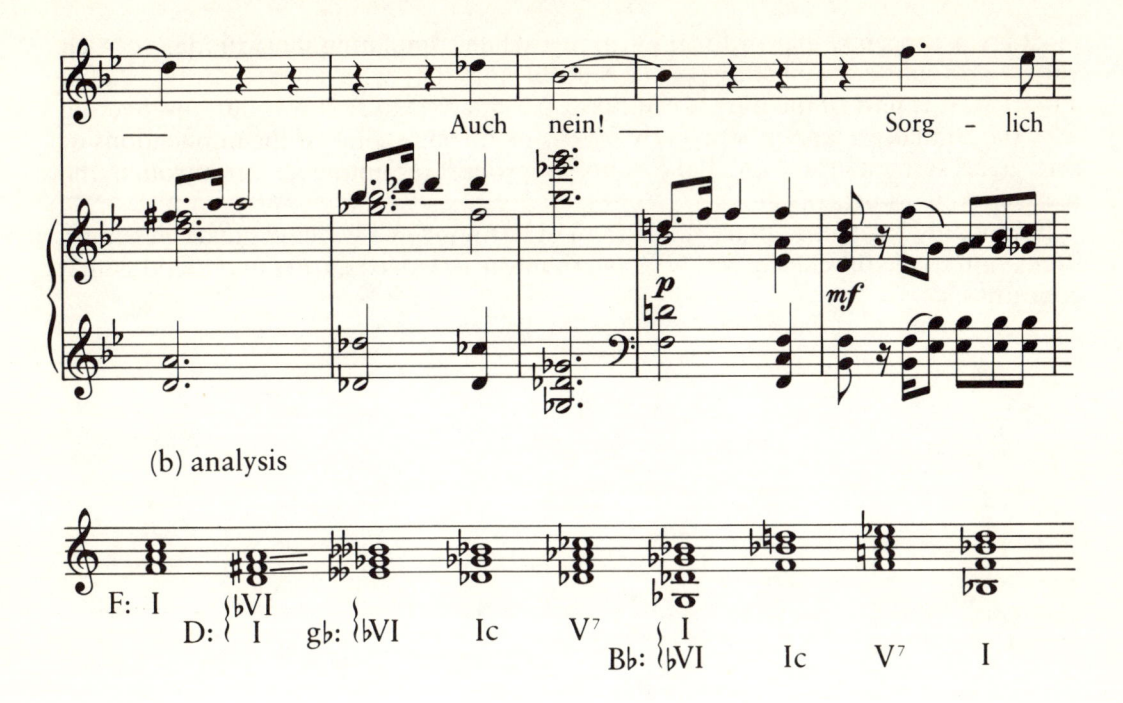

There is no need to catalogue the remaining chromatic chords, for they all follow the principles of chromatic inflection outlined in Chapter Four. It now only remains to place this vocabulary discussed in this chapter in a wider context, and view the phenomenon of tonal harmony in relation to the other elements of Western music as it was practised during the period which concerns us.

Our study has now reached the stage where it is appropriate to summarize the main principles of tonal harmony and thus put the work done so far into perspective.

Summary
Tonal harmony is based upon a hierarchy of chordal relationships in a given key, at the head of which stand the dominant and tonic chords. Just as the dominant is related to the tonic through the root movement of an upward 4th or downward 5th, so this dominant/tonic relationship can be extended to the remaining chords (as in the Cycle of 5ths), establishing a powerful harmonic syntax that underlies and gives coherence to many a richly chromatic passage. For, chromaticism in tonal harmony grows out of the diatonic processes according to a fundamental principle: all notes above the root of a chord may be chromatically inflected without altering the function of that chord. It is this which imparts a remarkable unity to what at first sight appears to be an array of unrelated chromatic chords. Another basic principle of tonal harmony is that every chord embodies a multiplicity of potential functions (or relationships) giving rise to seemingly infinite possibilities of modulation. Like

most great concepts, that of tonal harmony, while stimulating musical ideas of rich variety and subtle complexity, has a beautiful simplicity which is not always readily apparent. It is part of the purpose of harmonic analysis to seek this out, discovering how the composer, who in intuitively following through some of the implications of this great system, has turned the familiar procedures into real art through the mysterious workings of genius.

It now only remains to place this system of harmony in a wider context, viewing it in relation to the other elements of Western music practised during the period which concerns us.

Assignments for Chapter Five

1 (a) Play and memorize the following sequence. Transpose it into at least three other major keys. You should be able to sing any of the parts.

C: I   IV^7 vii^{ø7} iii^7 vi^7 ii^7 V^7 I

(b) Play and memorize the following sequence. Transpose it into B minor.

c: i   iv^7 ♭VII^7 III^7 VI^7 ii^{ø7} V^7 i

2 Continue the sequence of secondary 7ths as commenced by Vivaldi in the following extract, maintaining the distinctive pattern established in each part. Check your own working with Vivaldi's original, if possible.

Vivaldi: *Concerto Grosso, Op. 3, No. 10*

3 Using symbols under the bass stave, analyse the harmonic structure of the following passages. Circle the dissonant note in each secondary 7th and indicate the direction of its resolution with an arrow.

(a) Chorale: *O Ewigkeit du Donnerwort*

F:

(b) Chorale: *Allein zu dir, Herr Jesu Christ*

b:

(c) Beethoven: *Sonata in D, Op. 10, No. 3*

RONDO
Allegro

E♭

{ E♭
{ D

4 (a) Write the dominant minor 9th of the following keys: G major, G minor, F minor, C♯ minor, E♭ major, G♭ major. (Use key-signatures, and note that the dominant minor 9th is chromatic in major keys.)

(b) Strike out the root of each dominant minor 9th, and resolve the resulting diminished 7th to the tonic of each key. For example, in E major:

5   Analyse this chorale harmonization by J. S. Bach. Where diminished 7ths function as dominants indicate the missing root by ⋀ (placed on the correct line or space).

Chorale: O *Mensch schau Jesum Christum an*

g: d:

g: *etc.*

6   On the piano play the twelve resolutions of the four diminished 7th chords when they function as dominant minor 9ths. (These may resolve to either major or minor tonics.) Your left hand will supply what would be the 'missing root' resolving to the tonic. Sing each note in the right-hand chord, letting your ear guide its resolution. Thus:

etc.

7 Analyse the following extract using as a guide Ex.87 (p.94):

a:

8 Re-write the following passages, replacing the chord marked * with a chromatic dominant chord on the same degree of the scale,

e.g. ii – V changes to II – V – I.
(V of V)

Re-write the whole passage, not just the chord in question and add the appropriate analytical symbols, for example:

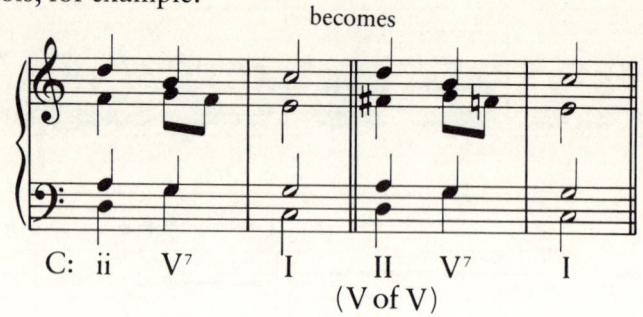

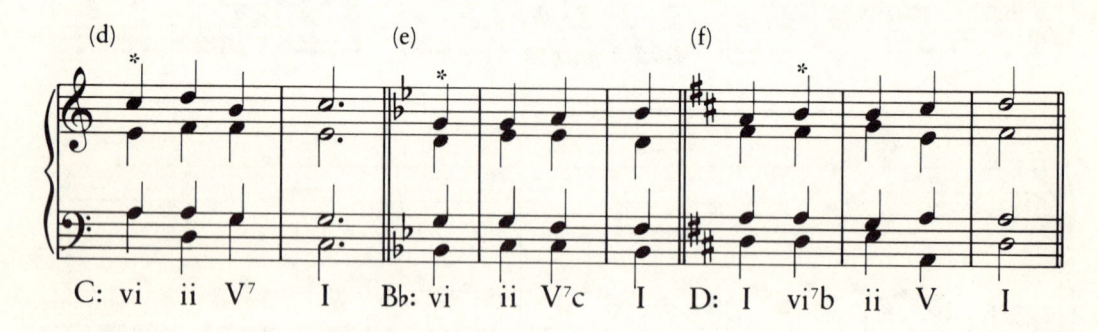

becomes

C: ii V⁷ I   II V⁷ I
            (V of V)

(a)   A: iib V I

(b)   F: vi ii⁷ V I

(c)   e: ii°b ic V i

(d)   C: vi ii V⁷ I

(e)   B♭: vi ii V⁷c I

(f)   D: I vi⁷b ii V I

(g)   C: I iii vi IV I

(h)   c: i III VI iv i

(i)   F: iiib vi ii⁷ V⁷ I

C: I IV I   c: i iv i   C: I iii vi vi ii V I

9 Analyse the following passages. Regard each one as being in the same key throughout and use the double symbolization when dealing with chromatic dominants, i.e. V of ii, etc.

(a) In this chorale quaver movement which brings a distinct change of harmony is indicated by an asterisk. Other passing quaver movement can be disregarded for the purposes of analysis.

Chorale: *Wenn wir in höchsten Nöten sein* (harm. J. S. Bach)

F:

(b) Beethoven: *Sonata in E♭, Op. 31, No. 3*

B♭:

(c) Mozart: *Piano Sonata in D, K284*

Var. X

D:

from here →

EXTENSIONS OF THE TRIADIC FOUNDATION 113

10 (a) Taking Ex.95 (p.99) as a model, trace the supertonic function of the following augmented 6th chords:

G: a: D♭:

(b) Trace the dominant function of the following augmented 6th chords:

C:

11 Analyse these extracts. Name the type of augmented 6th being used and also indicate its function.

(a) Schubert: *Der Zwerg*

Nicht zu geschwind

114   EXTENSIONS OF THE TRIADIC FOUNDATION

(b) Beethoven: *Sonata in E♭, Op. 31, No. 3*

12 (a)   Enharmonically change these German and Italian 6ths into dominant 7ths:

  (b)   Enharmonically change these dominant 7ths into German 6ths:

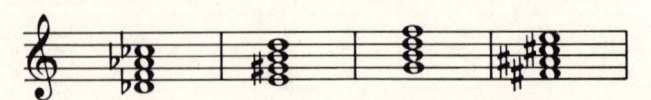

13   Analyse the following sequence and memorize it at the piano:

14   The following exercise is to help develop aural sensitivity towards the different harmonic forces at work on the melodic intervals of major 2nd and diminished 3rd when they are used in dominant 7th and Neapolitan 6th resolutions respectively. Analyse the sequence and sing it with the accompaniment.

15   Analyse Chopin's Prelude in C minor.

16 Analyse the following extract from Schubert's *Der Zwerg* which contains most of the chords discussed in Chapter Five.

Nicht zu geschwind

Ster - ben ein - zig mir noch Freu - de, ein - zig mir noch Freu - de Zwar werd' ich e - wig-lich mich sel - ber has - sen der dir mit die - ser Hand den Tod ge - ge - ben, doch musst zum frü - hen Grab du nun er - blas - - sen.

CHAPTER SIX
HARMONY IN STRUCTURAL CONTEXT

We now come to consider harmony in context with the other elements which contribute to musical structure and design. To illustrate this let us examine the Minuet from Mozart's Piano Sonata, K282.

EX.102 Mozart: *Piano Sonata in B♭ K282*

Menuetto I

It seems indisputable that much of the satisfaction we derive from the performance of music springs from the subtle and seemingly endless ways in which melody, phrasing, harmonic rhythm, texture, tempo, dynamics, harmony, etc, all interact. What is more, each of these elements can be appreciated from different 'perspectives', each perspective interacting with the others.

Take, for example, the question of phrasing, a term primarily associated with melodic shape. We can interpret the shape of Mozart's melody in a number of different ways:

EX.103

Brackets marked (a) break up the melody into its smallest units of construction, while brackets (b) and (c) fuse these into larger spans. As in speech where we are aware of individual words forming longer and longer ideas, so in music do we apprehend different spans of musical thought at the same time. Through various kinds of articulation (usually indicated by the composer) a performer may bring a particular span into greater prominence; yet we are intuitively aware of the others. In the example above Mozart has provided marks of articulation (slurs and staccato) which tend to bring some of the smaller units into prominence. Nevertheless we still comprehend their part in the larger context, and so it could be said that we appreciate the melody from different perspectives at the same time. Thus, not only do the elements of design interact, but they also interact at different 'levels'. Mozart's marks of articulation also contribute to the contrasts of rhythmic flow in this piece. Up to the end of bar 4 each idea has started with an anacrusis which brings the third beat of the bar into rhythmic focus. The slurs from bars 5 – 9 change this emphasis, resulting in a subtle contrast. Without Mozart's slurs the melody from this point onwards might well be shaped in a way that retains the anacrusis:

EX.104

It is clear that Mozart preferred the contrast.

These little points of detail are vastly important. They form the foreground of our musical experience. Our response to music however also takes in the background or the wider spans,[1] and analysis which does not take this into account lacks an essential dimension. An analysis of the widest span represents a kind of abstract (i.e. the 'essence') of the music's structure and probably requires more interpretative insight than does the analysis of the shorter spans for the reason that one has to go beyond the details to the structural principle. If we were, for example, to try and 'abstract' the structure of Mozart's melody we have to hear more than the little turns of phrase and those features which help impart character to it; we must search out the basic idea which these details decorate. The opening is clearly an embellishment of four descending notes:

EX.105

---

[1]For a study of this in relation to rhythm see Grosvenor Cooper and Leonard B. Meyer, *The Rhythmic Structure of Music* (University of Chicago Press, 1960). The authors use the term 'architectonic levels' to describe the different spans.

This is followed sequentially by another group of four descending notes. Now while the 5th bar could likewise be interpreted as an embellishment of yet another series of descending notes

EX.106

the impact of the harmony at this point (particularly through the bass pedal-point) and the change of phrasing and dynamics which brings the note F into repeated prominence suggests that bars 5 and 6 are merely decorative prolongations of F. Indeed, because of the sudden change of dynamics in the next bar, the note F seems to reveal itself as the structural point also of bar 7 before getting caught up in the scale passage down from E♭. Thus the structure of the 12 bars can be shown as

EX.107

So that such a structural analysis is not seen as a mere intellectual game play Ex.107 and follow it immediately by Ex.102. You should be able to hear whether or not one contains the 'essence' of the other. The mere exercise of attempting to aurally relate one to the other is useful for those whose ability in 'long-range' listening is relatively undeveloped.

It is possible to take the abstraction further. Some listeners may well perceive the first eight notes of Ex.107 as a long anacrusis to the high F, and the final two notes as a kind of coda, leaving the structure simply as a descending scale F to F. Indeed so many melodies can be reduced to a scale pattern, or part of one, we might reasonably consider that such a shape constitutes something of an archetype in Western music.

If we take the next section of Mozart's Minuet movement we see that its melodic structure takes its cue from the brief instance of chromaticism found in bar 8. From the double bar the melodic structure could be shown as

EX.108

(Here again it would be possible to regard the chromatic opening as a long anacrusis to D, a point that we will return to when considering the harmonic implications of the passage.)

Having looked at the large span, or background, let us return to the details of the foreground and examine the little units of construction which impart a sense of unity and organic growth to the melody, now being aware of the way they decorate the scale-like structures shown above.

As in most well-knit pieces the opening gesture of Mozart's Minuet contains the motive from which the thematic material grows, in this case a four-note figure. This motive and its variants are shown below.

EX.109

Turning now to harmonic considerations. First the foreground, or details. The key of B♭ major is clearly established at the outset by the alternating tonic and dominant chords, and by Ic (with its melodic decorations) at bars 5 – 7. The end of the first section reveals a clear shift towards the dominant key F major. But what an extraordinary way Mozart goes about this modulation. At bar 7 the key is unequivocally B♭. Mozart however deliberately leaves Ic up in the air and then thwarts our expectations of its resolution to V in the same key. Instead Ic in B♭ is followed by Ic in F.

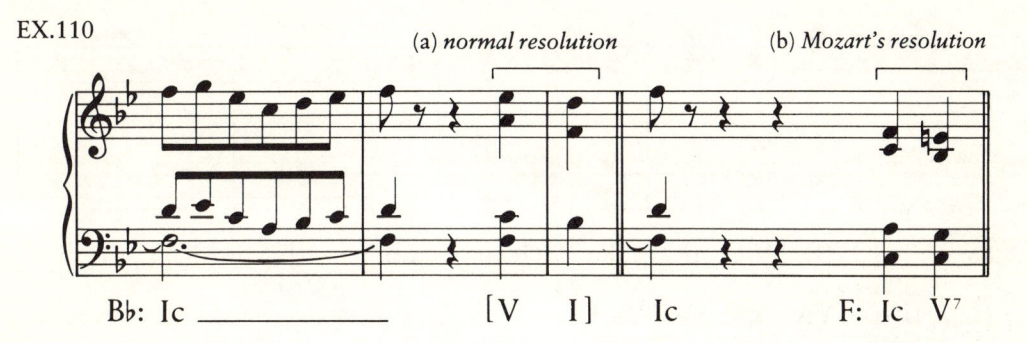

EX.110

(a) *normal resolution*   (b) *Mozart's resolution*

B♭: Ic ——————   [V I]   Ic   F: Ic V^7

The whole passage is made stranger by the touches of chromaticism in the descending melodic phrase linking the two 2nd inversion chords, especially the E♭ in the harmonic context of Ic in B♭ which is still ringing in our ears. Out of this curious instability and strangeness Mozart lunges into F major, the ruggedness of the move made more emphatic by the (subito) forte dynamics and the rhythmic shift which places an accent on the dotted figure which up until now bore the anacrusis. Now it has become the strong beat and the figure asserts a completely new and unexpectedly forceful character. How superbly has Mozart upset the courtly elegance of the opening bars, and how delightfully does it return – almost as if the courtier has been brought to order by a glance from his partner![1]

The contrast between bars 9 – 10 and all that has led up to them is further heightened by the change in harmonic rhythm. For the first time in the piece the harmony changes more rapidly than one chord per bar. This change is taken up in the next section which commences with a harmonic rhythm of three chord changes per bar during the span of chromatic harmony. The point is simply that music gains part of its unity through consistent harmonic rhythm, as well as variety through changes in harmonic rhythm. It is one of those musical elements which we absorb quite unconsciously, yet the part it plays is vital. So it contributes to the contrasting nature of the musical idea immediately following the double bar. So too does the change of texture – the arpeggiated chords – emphasize the contrast. Yet like most thematic contrasts in classical music the idea actually springs from material heard earlier, in this case (as we have already noted) from the chromatic step in bar 8.

---

[1] Although the 17th century minuet had been a fast, gay ballroom dance, by Mozart's time it had acquired a slower tempo and stately character.

After the unambiguous tonic/dominant harmonies in the first part of Mozart's piece, the second part seems for a moment to ruffle the clear tonality. The first chord indeed belongs neither to F major nor to B♭ major, although momentarily the passage seems to hover between both until the home key emerges strongly from the third bar, the chromatic supertonic chord clinching the key in a delectable false-relation.

EX.111

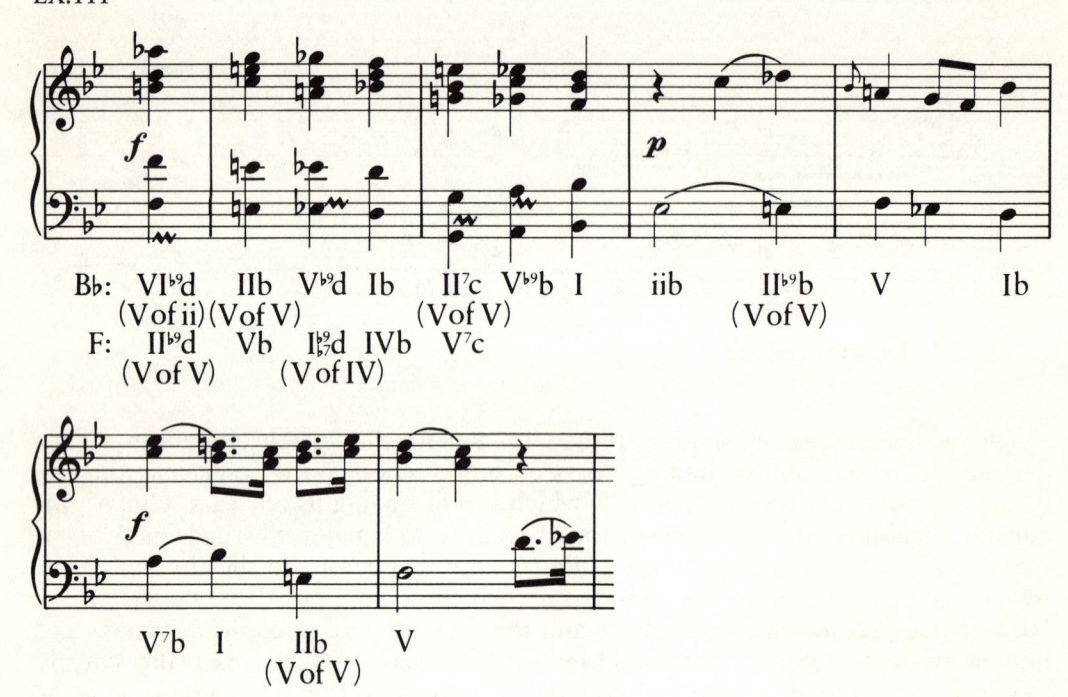

B♭:   VI♭⁹d   IIb   V♭⁹d Ib   II⁷c V♭⁹b I   iib   II♭⁹b   V   Ib
    (V of ii)(V of V)   (V of V)   (V of V)
F: II♭⁹d   Vb   I♭⁹₇d IVb   V⁷c
    (V of V)   (V of IV)

V⁷b I   IIb   V
          (V of V)

From there to the end of the piece the tonality remains firmly in B♭.

From the long-range view one can perceive the harmonic structure simply as an extension and decoration of the B♭ tonality. The focal points of the harmonic structure are:

  a) the establishment of key at the opening
  b) chords on the dominant at the end of the first section
  c) supertonic-dominant chords just before the return of the melody.

These all highlight the tonality. The chromatic chords at the beginning of the second section 'decorate' the tonality, giving point to its clear return. The following example incorporating both harmonic and melodic structures illustrates this long-range view.

EX.112

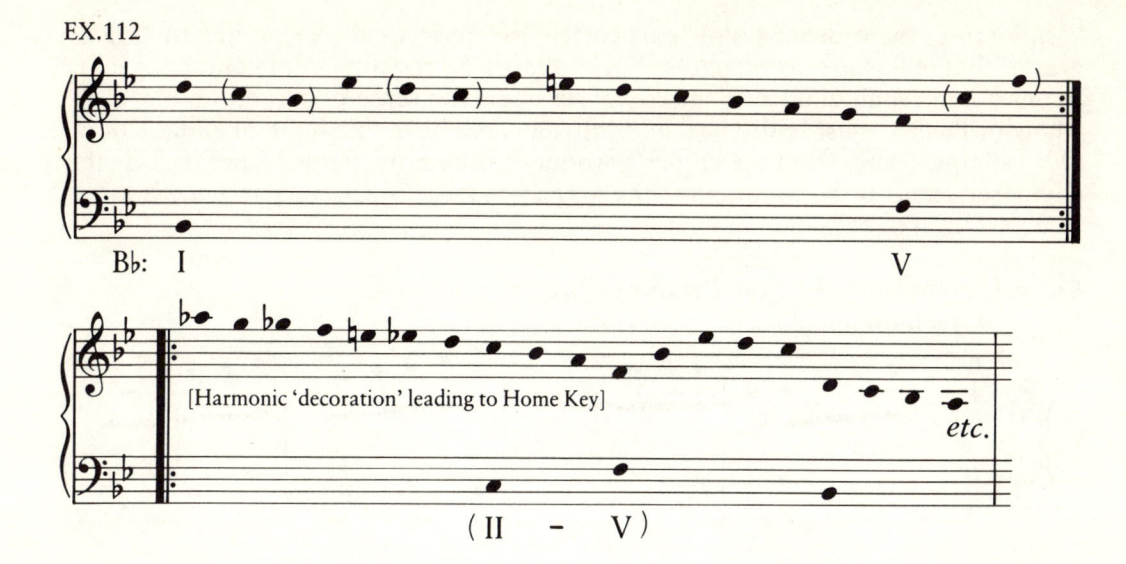

Bb: I   V

[Harmonic 'decoration' leading to Home Key]   *etc.*

(II   –   V)

Try to listen to the piece now in terms of 'background structure'.

Our study of Mozart's Minuet commenced by considering aspects of phrasing, and we shall conclude by returning briefly to this matter.

We saw how musical phrasing can be interpreted in different ways, from brief gestures to wide spans. Music from the 17th century onwards was greatly influenced by the dance, the supple, plastic rhythms of much renaissance vocal music giving way to a more regular and metrical style. Dance pieces, of course, are usually very symmetrical, their cadences marking off the periods every two or four bars. It is a sign of the sophistication of Mozart's style in this piece that such regularity is broken. After the symmetry of the opening the music seems to take wing in the two six-bar phrases.

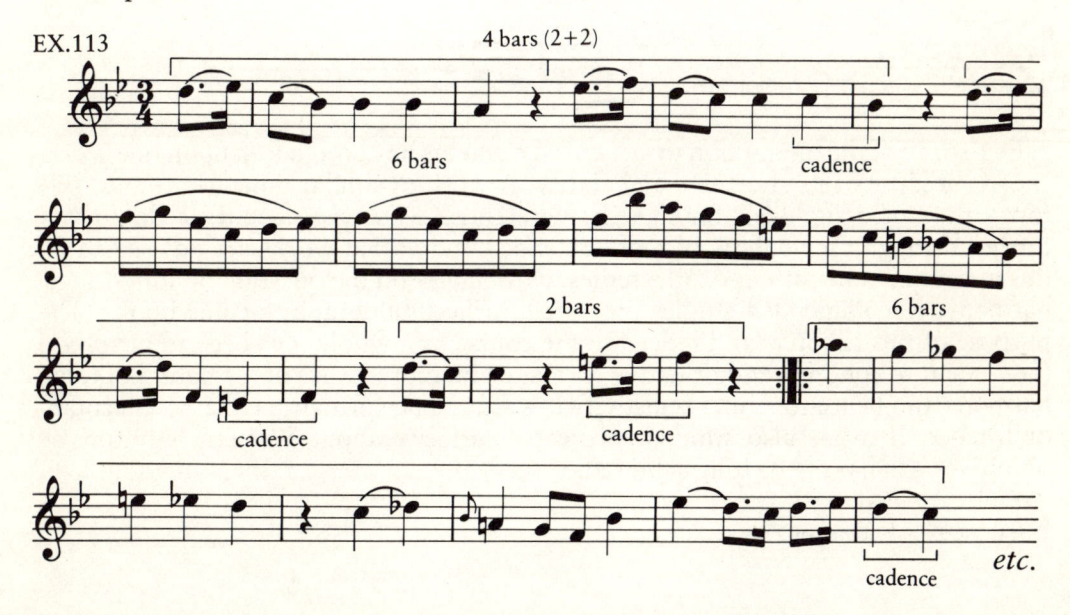

EX.113

In a sense, the cadence-point (particularly the perfect cadence) is like the tug of gravity that pulls the soaring phrase back to earth. By resisting it, or concealing it (as in much contrapuntal music), the composer imparts a sense of breadth to his ideas. Many of Bach's arias, both vocal and instrumental, have this sense of endless flow. Our example comes from the French baroque. Notice how in this 13 bar melody the composer seems to be fighting off the perfect cadence to the very last, with just a brief respite at bars 7 – 8.

EX.114 Clérambault: *Air from Pyrâme et Thisbé*

Our study of the interaction of structural elements has been based upon one work, chosen because of its shortness and clarity. A work of similar dimensions and style forms the one assignment for this chapter. Those who wish to pursue the matter further through the analysis of more extended and varied works are advised to do this in conjunction with in-depth studies, particularly on the question of 'long-range' harmony. Recommended studies are listed in the Bibliography of this book.[1] The purpose of this chapter (and indeed of the course as a whole) has been to *introduce* the student to concepts and practices; to make him more aware of the nature of tonal harmony and hence to a finer sensitivity towards its performance either as executant or listener. If it has also stimulated greater curiosity about Western harmony its objectives will have been fully achieved.

[1] See those by Salzer and by Forte.

Assignment for Chapter Six

Analyse the following work along the lines suggested in Chapter Six, taking into account harmonic, melodic, rhythmic, motivic and textural elements, as well as considering the part played in the overall structure by harmonic rhythm and phrasing. Try to distinguish between harmonic and melodic 'foreground' and 'background'.

Haydn: *Piano Sonata in F, Hob. XVI/29*

FURTHER READING

R. F. Goldman, *Harmony in Western Music* (New York, Norton, 1965)
W. Piston, *Principles of Harmonic Analysis* (New York, Schirmer, 1933)
W. Piston, *Harmony,* 4th edition revised and expanded by M. Devoto (New York, Norton, 1978)
E. E. Lowinsky, *Tonality and Atonality in 16th century Music* (University of California Press, 1961)
R. R. Reti, *Tonality, Atonality and Pantonality* (London, Rockcliff, 1958)
H. Schenker, *Harmony* (University of Chicago Press, 1954, rep. 1964)
H. Schenker, *Five Graphic Music Analyses* (New York, Dover Publications, 1969)
A. Forte and S. Gilbert, *Introductiion to Schenkerian Analysis* (New York, Norton, 1982)
F. Salzer, *Structural Hearing – Tonal Coherence in Music* (New York, Dover Publications, 1962)
G. Cooper and L. B. Meyer, *The Rhythmic Structure of Music* (University of Chicago Press, 1960)